Praise for *How to Get Divorced Without Losing Your Blouse*

"How to Get Divorced Without Losing Your Blouse is a comprehensive book that every woman must consult on their way through the divorce maze."

— Faydra Koenig, America's Divorce Coach

"How to Get Divorced Without Losing Your Blouse is a superb guidebook for women to plan for their future when facing divorce. It provides clear, concise answers to commonly asked questions so they know what to expect and that can lead to better decisions."

—Harmon W. Caldwell, Jr., Attorney at Law, Caldwell, Propst & DeLoach, LLP

"It helps your case to be an informed client! Reading this guide is the first step. It is concise, well-written and informative. It will help you formulate your questions for your lawyer."

— Emily Brenner, Esq., Brenner Law Group, LLC

MINDING YOUR MONEY

How to Get DIVORCED Without Losing Your Blouse

What Every Woman Needs to Know to Protect Her Future

PATRICIA A. STALLWORTH

PS Worth Publishing

Copyright © 2017 by Patricia A. Stallworth

All rights reserved. No part of this book may be reproduced, stored in a retrieval system, or transmitted in any form or by any means, including electronic, mechanical, photocopying, recording, or any information storage and retrieval system – except in the case of brief quotations used in critical articles or reviews – without the prior written permission of the publisher and the author.

ISBN: 978-0978550240

Published by PS Worth Publishing

Bulk discounts available. For more information, contact: info@psworth.com

DISCLAIMER: Although the author and publisher have made every effort to ensure that the information in this book was correct at the time of publication, the author and publisher do not assume and hereby disclaim any liability to any party for any loss, damage, disruption caused by errors or omissions, whether such errors or omissions result from negligence, accident, or any other cause. This book is not to be considered a substitution for legal advice. It is sold with the understanding that neither the author nor the publisher is engaged in rendering legal or other professional advice or services. If such legal or other expert assistance is required, the services of a competent professional should be sought. No professional advice can be given to any reader without the professional's full knowledge and analysis of the particular facts and circumstances.

HOW TO GET DIVORCED WITHOUT LOSING YOUR BLOUSE Worksheets & Checklists

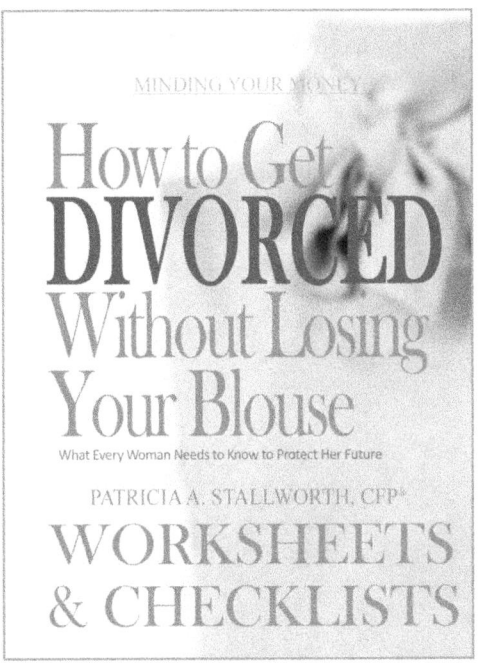

Download full-sized copies to complete and share with your divorce team.

www.psworth.com/divorce

*For all my mothers, sisters and daughters
who must travel on the road to divorce…
stay strong…this too shall pass.*

CONTENTS

INTRODUCTION
    IF YOU'RE GETTING DIVORCED… YOU OWE IT TO
    YOURSELF TO GET PREPARED 1
    WHAT'S INSIDE 3

CHAPTER 1
    OVERVIEW OF THE LEGAL PROCESS 6

CHAPTER 2
    SEPARATION AGREEMENTS 16

CHAPTER 3
    PROPERTY AND DEBTS 24

CHAPTER 4
    PENSIONS AND RETIREMENT PLANS 38

CHAPTER 5
    SOCIAL SECURITY 44

CHAPTER 6
    ALIMONY 48

CHAPTER 7
    CHILD CUSTODY AND SUPPORT 54

CHAPTER 8
    INSURANCE AND TAXES 59

CHAPTER 9
    CHOOSING AN ATTORNEY 64

EPILOGUE
    PERSONAL DIVORCE PLANNING 101 71

APPENDIX A: THE WORKBOOK 77

APPENDIX B: GLOSSARY 132

APPENDIX C: RESOURCES..138

ABOUT MINDING YOUR MONEY

ABOUT THE AUTHOR

THANK YOU!

Message to Readers

This book is interactive! To bring it to life simply scan the QR (quick response) codes with your smartphone or tablet to watch videos that were created especially for you.

How to Scan the QR Codes in this Book

Step 1: Download a free QR code reader onto your smartphone or tablet from your App Store. I selected the Kaywa Reader because it is free of advertisements.

Step 2: Tap the app once it is downloaded to your phone; this will open the Reader. Tap again and your camera will automatically will appear to be on. Hover over the code you wish to scan and the camera will take a picture of the QR code; then your phone will be directed to a web page on psworth.com that contains each video message.

Enjoy!

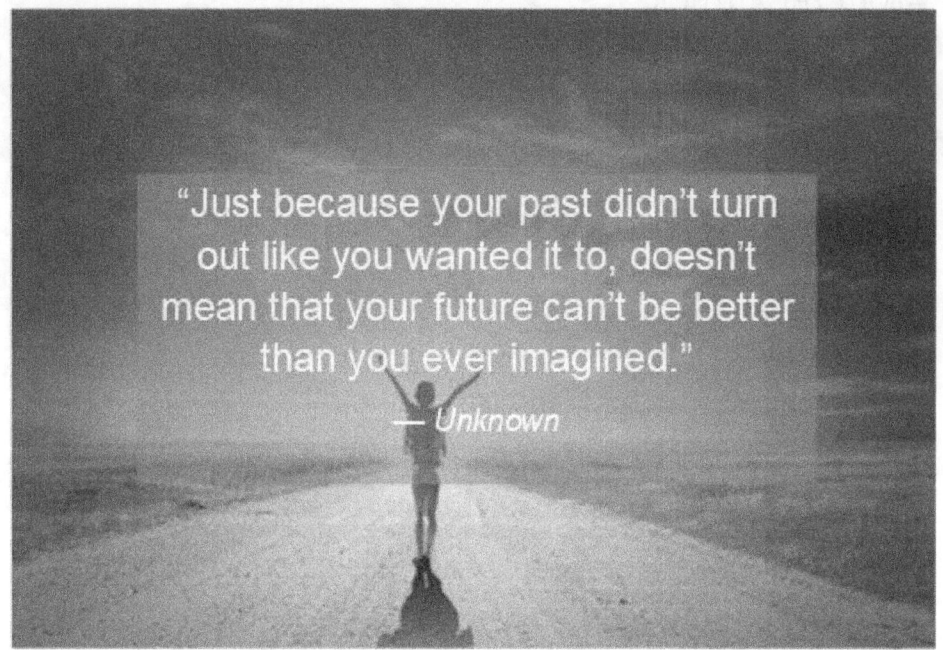

Watch Video Message: Patricia Stallworth - Welcome!

www.psworth.com/divorcebook

INTRODUCTION

IF YOU'RE GETTING DIVORCED... YOU OWE IT TO YOURSELF TO GET PREPARED

"Just because your past didn't turn out like you wanted it to, doesn't mean your future can't be better than you ever imagined." — Unknown

Fairy tales have happy endings. The prince swoops in, rescues the princess and they live happily ever after. But divorce is not a fairy tale and there is no prince charming that's coming to rescue you. In fact, the opposite is often true. Divorce can be devastating *even when it's the best solution*. It's emotionally draining and it's often financially draining as well, especially if you don't understand the process and what you can do to protect your future.

I know this because I've been there. I was there when my prince charming turned into my biggest adversary and said and did things I would never have imagined. And, because I didn't know any better, I made a lot of mistakes. I didn't understand how it all worked, what I was supposed to do, and more importantly, the impact it would have on my life for years. In short, I let the process control me instead of the other way around and as a result, I learned a lot of lessons the hard way.

The problem is, divorce messes with your mind and your emotions and it can send you on a virtual roller coaster ride. One day you're high, feeling okay and then so low the next day that you would do almost anything just to make it stop.

Unfortunately, this is also when lots of important decisions have to be made—decisions that can affect your life for a very long time. But, it's so easy to get overwhelmed and get caught up in everything that's going on around you that it's difficult to know what to do or how to respond to all of the questions that are constantly coming at you. As a result, many women (and some men too) don't always make the best decisions regarding money and their future.

I have witnessed first-hand some of the tragedies that can occur when women are not prepared for the divorce process. Sadly, many don't even realize that they have made poor decisions for months after their divorce when the consequences of their actions or non-actions during their divorce process become their reality.

Today, as a financial coach I help clients avoid many of the mistakes I (and others) made so they can make better decisions for their lives whether they are going through a divorce, planning for retirement or they just want to use their money to live better lives today.

I wrote *How to Get Divorced Without Losing Your Blouse: 129 Things Every Woman Needs to Know to Protect Her Future* because despite the fact that divorce affects nearly one-half of all marriages, it's still surrounded by a shroud of secrecy that makes the process more difficult and scary because you just don't know what to expect. And, I designed it to specifically fill that knowledge gap so you know what to expect and can be better prepared.

Knowledge, after all, is power and if you're getting a divorce, whether it's your idea or not, you owe it to yourself to be prepared!

ps!

WHAT'S INSIDE

How to Get Divorced Without Losing Your Blouse walks you through the divorce process and provides answers to basic questions you are likely to encounter along the way. It was written to assist those who are contemplating, anticipating or going through divorce. The information presented here is meant to be a starting point to learn about the process, resources you can use and various options available to you, so you can be an informed participant in the process. However, since everyone's situation is different, be prepared to conduct additional research related to your specific case.

How to Get Divorced Without Losing Your Blouse is based on some of the most frequently asked questions clients have asked me over the years. It's written in a Q&A format so it is an easy read and it's organized into ten chapters. The chapters range from a general overview of the divorce process to specific questions related to dividing your finances, and it includes a bonus chapter on personal divorce planning to help you mentally prepare for the process.

It also includes worksheets, checklists and resources so you know the types of information you will need to have available throughout the process and where to get additional information if necessary.

Finally, it serves as a resource guide to help you stay on track and ensure that you are covering the areas that are important for your future financial health.

So, let's get started!

READ THIS FIRST: As you read through the following questions, it is important to understand that this is written in general terms and should be used as a guide, and for informational purposes only. Each state may use different terms and/or handle divorce issues a bit differently, so check with a local attorney or review your state's laws for specifics in your area. Use the Resources section in Appendix G for contact information and links to divorce laws, state bar associations, and legal and financial professionals.

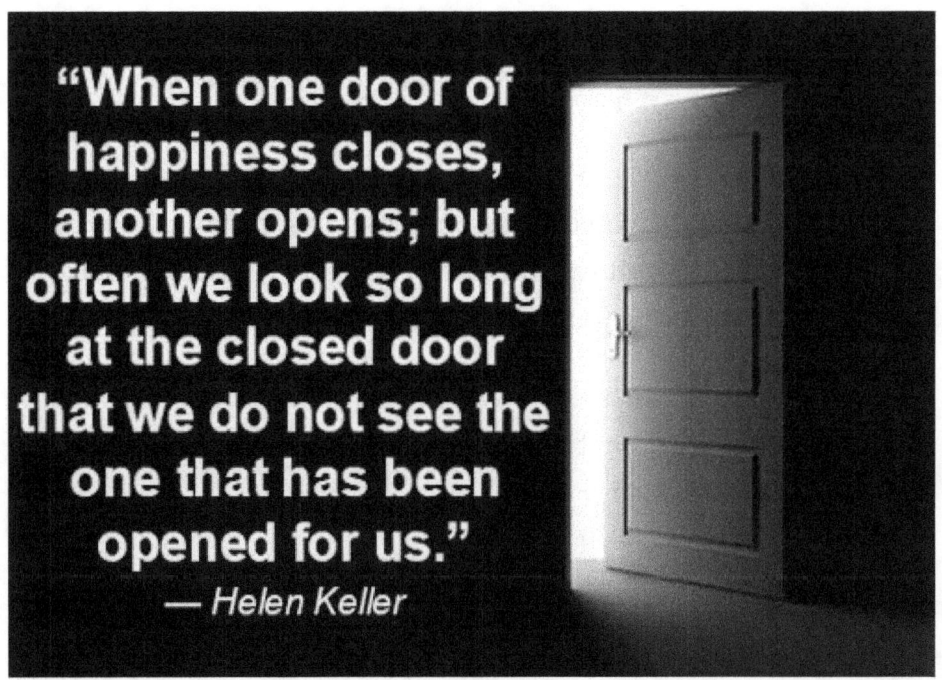

Watch Video Message: Patricia Stallworth - Chapter 1 Intro

www.psworth.com/divorcechapters

CHAPTER 1

OVERVIEW OF THE LEGAL PROCESS

"When one door of happiness closes, another opens; but often we look so long at the closed door that we do not see the one that has been opened for us." — Helen Keller

For many people a divorce represents their first dealings with the court and court procedures so this can be a scary process even without all of the other stuff that's going on.

Chapter 1 provides an overview of the divorce process so you will have a better idea of what to expect so the process becomes less intimating and less scary.

---

1. **What is a divorce?** A divorce is a civil action to terminate a marriage. It is also called a Dissolution of Marriage.

2. **Do we both have to file for divorce?** Only one spouse needs to file. However, if he/she wishes the other spouse can file a counter claim. The person who files is called the Petitioner or Plaintiff. The spouse who is served is called the Respondent or Defendant.

3. **What generally happens during the divorce process?**
In most cases, a divorce begins when one spouse files a Petition or Complaint for divorce. The Petition includes what that spouse is asking for, such as child custody, property divisions, or alimony. Petition papers are then served or delivered to the other spouse, and he/she has the option to respond.

While the case is pending, if necessary, either spouse can ask the court to make an immediate decision on temporary orders for matters such as child custody, visitation, living arrangements, how assets will be handled, and if needed, restraining orders. Also, if you are represented by lawyers, they will begin to gather information from both spouses regarding assets and debts, as well as employment, in preparation for the final settlement.

Next, the settlement process begins. During this time, spouses decide how to settle issues such as the division of their assets and debts, the care and custody of their children, and any financial arrangements, such as child support and alimony. The settlement process can be completed informally between the spouses or more formally through negotiation, mediation, arbitration or a court trial, and involve lawyers, judges, mediators, arbitrators, family therapists, or financial professionals.

The final step is the divorce decree, which spells out the details of the divorce settlement agreement and formally ends the marriage.

4. **What are the grounds for filing for divorce?**
Although the terms used vary from state to state, most states permit divorce for "irreconcilable differences,"

"incompatibility" or those that are "irretrievably broken." In other words, a no-fault divorce.

5. **What is a "no-fault" divorce?** No-fault divorce laws allow spouses to divorce without assigning blame or fault to the other spouse. To use no-fault as grounds for divorce, one spouse must simply state that the marriage is not salvageable.

6. **What is a fault-based divorce?** In a fault-based divorce one spouse assigns blame to the other for the failure of the marriage because of some type of marital misconduct. Common reasons for fault-based divorces include adultery, physical or mental cruelty, desertion, and alcohol or drug abuse.

7. **Are there advantages to filing a fault-based divorce?** There are some instances where more assets and/or alimony have been awarded to the innocent spouse. Also, it may also be helpful in some child custody cases.

However, the downside to fault-based divorce cases is that they tend to be more costly and take longer to settle. So, before you file a fault-based divorce case, try to find out if there are any advantages in your specific situation. Speak with an attorney, or do some research in your area to determine the outcome of similar cases.

8. **What if my spouse won't give me a divorce?** There's really no way that one spouse can give — or not give — the other spouse a divorce. They may not like the idea or want it, but they don't have the power to stop it. By its very nature, divorce is not a thing—it's a process. As long as you can prove your legal grounds (reasons), a judge will grant you a final judgment, which officially ends the marriage.

9. **What is an uncontested divorce?** An uncontested divorce is one where the spouses agree on everything and do not need the court to divide assets or make determinations about spousal or child support or custody. In general, an uncontested divorce will proceed through the system more quickly, and be much less costly.

10. **What are temporary orders?** Temporary orders spell out what happens between the time the divorce papers are filed and when the divorce is granted regarding child custody, child support, visitation, alimony, living arrangements, how assets will be handled, etc., and if needed, restraining orders.

11. **What are permanent orders?** Permanent orders are issued by the court at the end of divorce negotiations when the divorce is final.

12. **What should be included in a final divorce decree?** Your divorce decree should include everything that you need to completely protect your rights in the areas of the process itself, property divisions, alimony, and child custody and support. *(See Appendix E for a complete checklist.)*

13. **Who chooses which settlement method my spouse and I use and who pays for it?** This answer varies from state to state. For example, mediation is a requirement in some states. Beyond any state mandated requirements, you and your spouse are free to use any of the methods including negotiation, mediation, arbitration, a court trial or a combination of these. Of these, negotiation and mediation tend to be the least costly and offer you the most control over the outcome.

Each spouse is generally responsible for his/her share of the expenses, including court costs and any fees for professionals they hire. Exceptions to this are court mandated arrangements or those agreed upon by the spouses.

14. **What is mediation?** Mediation is a settlement process where a neutral third party assists spouses in reaching an agreement.

The role of the mediator is to facilitate or assist communication between spouses and to offer suggestions. Mediators do not make decisions, and they do not give legal advice. When choosing a mediator, select someone who is skilled in the major issues you need to resolve, such as child custody or the division of large assets.

Mediation is most effective when spouses are able to talk with each other and they are each able to stand up for their own rights. This process may be conducted with or without the use of attorneys. However, if you have an attorney, it is a good idea to have him/her review any agreements before you sign them. Decisions made during mediation are not final unless you sign off on them.

15. **What is arbitration?** In arbitration, each spouse presents his/her case to an arbitrator. The arbitrator then makes a settlement decision much like that of a judge. In most cases, this decision is binding (final) and not subject to appeal. Therefore, to get the best result, as with a mediator, you should choose an arbitrator who has worked with cases similar to yours. Even though you give up control over the outcome, arbitration is often a good alternative to a court trial because it can be a less costly, easier and a much quicker process.

16. **What is the court trial process like?** A court trial is a formal process that includes data gathering procedures such as depositions, discovery and the actual trial itself. During the court proceedings, there will be opening arguments and closing arguments by your attorneys as well as direct and cross examination of witnesses, including expert witnesses called by each side. Then the court will make its ruling.

17. **What is a deposition?** A deposition is testimony in preparation for a court trial. It is generally held outside of the courtroom. In addition to the person testifying, both attorneys and a court reporter are generally present.

18. **What is discovery?** Discovery is the process of obtaining information, including documents from the other side such as employment, benefits and banking and investment information.

19. **Isn't it always better to have a court trial?** In most cases, no. Divorce cases only end up in court when they cannot be resolved using any of the other settlement methods. A court trial is generally the most expensive option and it offers you the least amount of control over the final result. During a court trial, the judge or jury listens to your case and decides the issues for the final settlement agreement. Their ruling is generally final. Only a small percentage of divorce cases go to trial.

20. **What if I have a court trial and I don't agree with the Judge's ruling?** In most cases, the judge's ruling is final. However, depending on the state, there may be an appeal process. If a court trial is something you are considering, be sure to discuss whether or not there is an appeal process in your state with your attorney before you choose this option so you can make an informed decision.

21. **Am I required to have a lawyer?** No. However, unless you have a very simple divorce case, such as a short-term marriage, no children, no assets to divide, and you are both financially independent, it is recommended that you have legal representation even if only to get a second opinion before you sign any papers or agree to anything. This is *not* the best time to make decisions without getting advice and assistance from the professionals. If cost is an issue, think long-term and weigh the costs against the possible future benefits or losses.

Note: See Chapter 9 for more information on choosing an attorney and Appendix G for resources to locate lawyers in your area and free legal aid options.

22. **Can my spouse and I share an attorney?** While it may be a tempting idea. NO. One of the main reasons to hire an attorney is to have an advocate for you—someone looking out for *your interests*—and if you share an attorney with your spouse whose interests will they really be looking out for?

23. **How long will it take to get divorced?** Each state has an established waiting period that generally begins after the Petition or Complaint has been served. This is the shortest period of time you must wait before your divorce is final. However, this assumes that you and your spouse are in agreement on how to handle all of the issues. If this is not true in your case, you will need to allow more time. The amount of additional time will depend on how complex the issues are in your situation. For example, situations where you have a lot of assets, child custody issues and you and your spouse are unable to talk to each other directly can significantly lengthen the process.

24. **Can I resume the use of my maiden name at the time of the divorce?** Yes. However, this is not automatic. You must either file a request to resume your maiden name in your divorce papers or request information for resumption of your maiden name once the divorce is granted through your County Clerk's Office.

RECAP

The divorce process has three main parts: the filing, the settlement process and the final divorce decree. How quickly or slowly you move through the process is largely dependent on how long it takes you to resolve settlement issues.

Even though you might want the whole process to be over as quickly as possible, I would caution you to take enough time to understand what you want and why it's important to you. Don't fall into the trap of just settling for just anything to end it — this strategy rarely works in your favor.

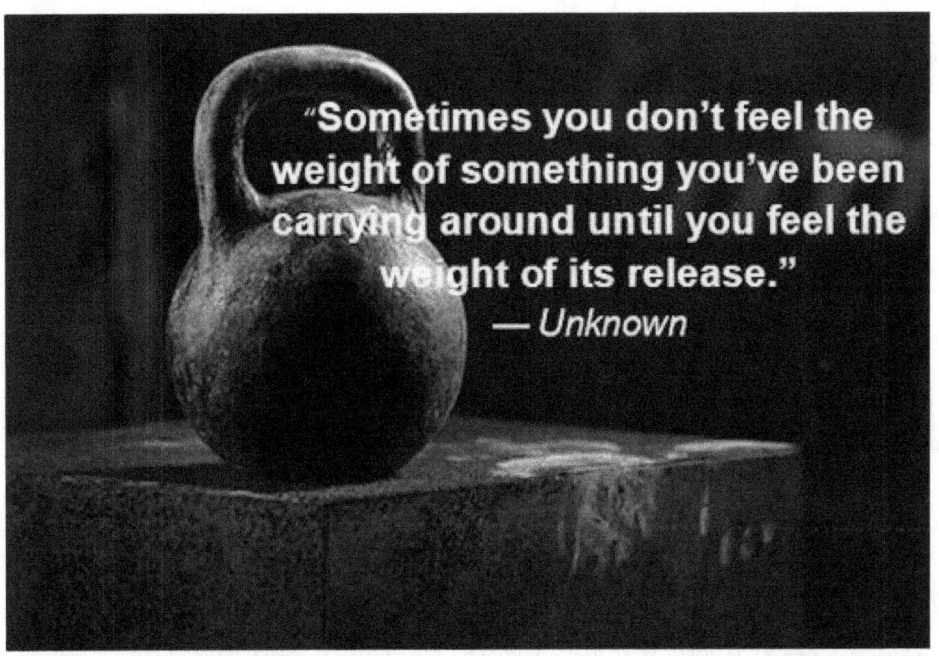

Watch Video Message: Patricia Stallworth - Chapter 2 Intro

www.psworth.com/divorcechapters

CHAPTER 2

SEPARATION AGREEMENTS

"Sometimes you don't feel the weight of something you've been carrying around until you feel the weight of its release." — Unknown

Sometimes couples decide to separate when they are having problems or contemplating a divorce. In some cases, they want time apart to work out some issues but eventually plan to get back together. However, in other cases, they know that they don't want to live together but they don't want to divorce either for financial, religious or other reasons. Unlike a divorce, a separation agreement does not end the marriage but you can use it to spell out your rights and help protect your interests.

Chapter 2 focuses on questions related to a legal separation to help you decide if this is a viable option in your situation.

---

25. **What is a legal separation agreement?** A legal separation agreement, also known as a marital or property settlement agreement is a written contract that allows couples to live apart, resolve issues such as dividing property and debts, alimony and child custody and support without actually dissolving the marriage.

Note: States treat legal separation agreements differently. Some require a legal separation before you can file for a divorce. Some recognize a legal separation but do not require it while others neither require nor recognize legal separation. So, check the specific details for your state before you select this option and start the process.

26. **Why choose a separation over a divorce?** There are several reasons. For example, some states require a separation before you can file for a divorce. However, even when this is not the case, you may still want to consider a legal separation if:

- You and/or spouse are not emotionally ready for a divorce
- You don't want to live together but do not want a divorce either for religious or other reasons
- You want to retain medical insurance, government or tax benefits that may continue because you are still considered to be married even though you are living separate lives.

Note: Choosing to have a legally binding marriage separation agreement is not necessarily faster or less expensive than filing for a divorce. Consider consulting with an attorney to help you review your options.

27. **What's the purpose of a legal separation agreement?** Although separating can have benefits, it can also have risks. For example, if you separate, you still remain liable for your spouse's debts and legal issues even though you are not living together. A written separation agreement can address some of these issues by providing for indemnification or limiting your liability for debts incurred by your spouse while you are separated. *Note:* If your spouse does not follow the terms of the agreement, you could incur additional court costs to enforce it.

In general, a separation agreement should detail terms such as:

- How you will share or divide marital assets and debts
- How joint credit cards will be handled
- How assets acquired during the separation will be distributed
- Your access to liquid assets (checking, savings, etc.) to pay bills.

Another important reason to have a separation agreement is that without one, you may not receive your share of the marital assets like investments, for example, as these may be lost or depleted during the separation.

28. **Do I need an attorney to draft a separation agreement?** Although you can write an agreement on your own, remember it can affect your life for a long time, and some of the questions and issues are complicated (like taxes) so it might be in your best interest to have an attorney prepare an agreement for you or at least review yours before you sign it.

29. **What if my spouse won't sign it?** If your spouse refuses to sign it then you have no agreement. A separation agreement is only good if both spouses sign it.

30. **Are there some don'ts regarding separation agreements that I should be aware of?** Yes. Here are some examples:

   a. Don't sign an agreement prepared by your spouse's attorney without having an independent attorney review it.

   b. Don't be in such a hurry that you don't take the time to think about your specific situation, your needs, and the needs of your children if you are a parent. Keep in mind that if you decide to divorce, this document could become the basis for your divorce settlement so consider your future as well before you sign an agreement.

31. **How long does a separation agreement last?** A separation agreement can be in effect indefinitely. However, you and your spouse can amend the agreement at any time if you both consent to the changes. And, the court can always modify provisions in an agreement regarding the care and custody of any minor children.

32. **Do the courts review the fairness of a settlement agreement?** Generally, in the case of an uncontested divorce, the court nearly always approves the agreement of the parties if it is generally fair and the court is convinced that the agreement was entered into by both spouses without fraud or coercion. Often the court may want to review financial affidavits attached to the agreement in order to determine its fairness. And, the courts may always weigh in on child custody matters and the amount allocated for support.

Note: Never agree to anything that you are not prepared to live with because your settlement agreement may become your final divorce decree if you decide to get divorced.

33. **Does a separation agreement help me get a divorce?** It could. Some states have provisions in their laws that could make your divorce faster or easier if there is a separation agreement in place.

34. **Can my spouse and I specify our child custody arrangement in our separation agreement?** For the most part, you may. However, some states do not allow separation agreements regarding the issues of child custody. Instead, they require an additional agreement concerning custody called a 'Parenting Plan Agreement' which details the custody arrangements. In most cases, you are permitted to outline the custody arrangements in the separation agreement and incorporate or merge it with the parenting plan agreement.

35. **If we spell out our child support arrangement in our separation agreement, does the judge have to accept it?** No, the judge is not bound by your agreement. If he or she finds that the agreement is unfair, unreasonable, inadequate, illegal, or subject to fraud, he or she can set it aside. Child support is very crucial to the future of the children and the judge will require an appropriate amount based upon issues like income, potential income, expenses, and visitation, which are normal variables in all child support guidelines.

36. **Can we decide who would claim the tax exemption for our children in our separate agreement?** Yes. The general rule is that the parent who has custody for more than half the year (the custodial parent) can claim the exemption. However, the custodial parent can allow the non-custodial parent to take the exemption by signing IRS Form 8332. The non-custodial parent can then attach Form 8332 to his or her tax return and claim the exemption. One parent can always claim the exemption or they can switch back and forth from year to year, but each child can only be claimed by one parent each year—you cannot split the exemption.

37. **Will a separation agreement free me from paying debts I signed for along with my spouse?** No. A separation agreement is only an agreement among spouses. It cannot bind third parties such as banks and financial institutions. However, if your spouse agrees to pay the debts and does not, so that you are held responsible, you can sue him/her for breach of contract.

38. **Will a separation agreement stop my spouse from harassing me?** Separation agreements generally don't have non-harassment clauses.

Note: If you are in a abusive relationship, you should seek the assistance of law enforcement to file the appropriate paperwork. A separation agreement is not the way to handle this situation.

RECAP

Separation agreements can be an alternative to divorce if you know you don't want a divorce for financial, religious or other reasons, or you are unsure if you really want one.

Having a formal contract in place allows you to mitigate some of the risks by spelling out resolutions to issues like property division, debts, alimony, child custody and support while still allowing you to take advantage of financial savings such as filing joint tax returns, access to health care, meeting the 10-year marriage requirement for Social Security, etc. because you are still legally married.

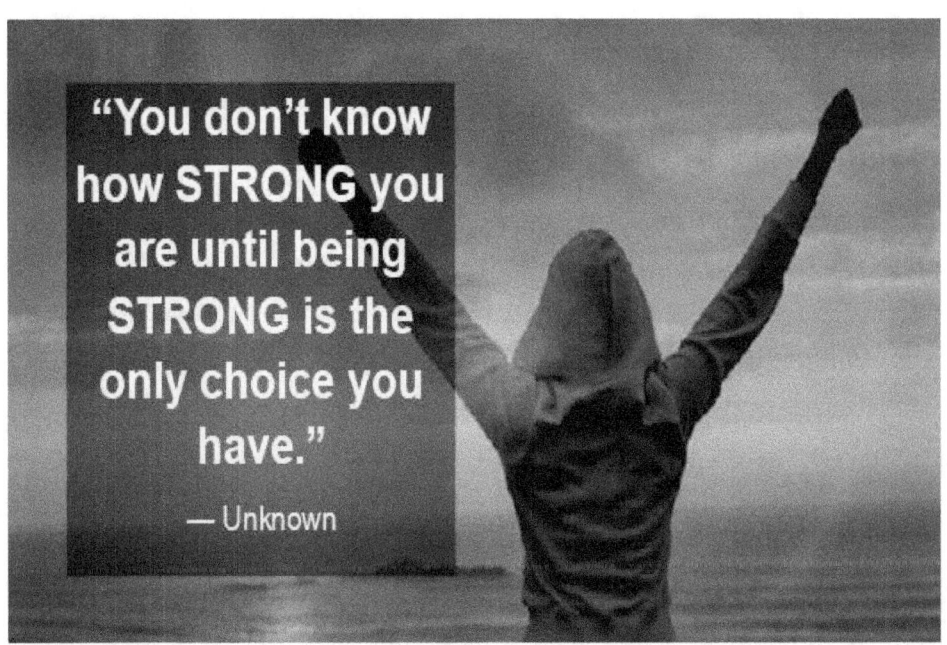

Watch Video Message: Patricia Stallworth - Chapter 3 Intro

www.psworth.com/divorcechapters

CHAPTER 3

PROPERTY AND DEBTS

"You don't know how STRONG you are until being STRONG is the only choice you have." — Unknown

There are two basic types of property — property acquired before the marriage and property acquired during the marriage. In general, property acquired during the marriage is considered marital property and subject to division regardless of which spouse owns the property or how it is titled.

Chapter 3 focuses on questions related to dividing your property and debts during a divorce settlement.

---

39. **What is property?** Property includes assets such as the family home, cars, bank accounts, stocks, bonds, retirement accounts, rental property, etc.

40. **What types of property are there?** Although the details vary from state to state, property generally falls into two categories: separate and marital.

41. **What is marital property?** Marital property is property acquired during the marriage regardless of whose name it's in. And, in some states it also includes the increase in value of separate property during the marriage.

42. **What is separate property?** There are three basic types of separate property:

- Property you bring into the marriage
- Property you inherit during the marriage
- Property you receive during the marriage as a gift

Note: Spending marital money, to improve a non-marital asset could create a partial marital interest in that asset. At a minimum, the value of the improvement is likely to be considered marital property. Courts often distinguish between active and passive appreciation of an asset.

Passive appreciation occurs when the non-marital asset increases in value without any action on your part. In other words, passive appreciation occurs when an asset goes up in value without adding any money or making improvements to it such as a stock that becomes more valuable over time.

Active appreciation occurs when the value of a non-marital asset increases because of an act or improvement to it by either party in the marriage. Active appreciation of a non-marital asset can create a marital interest in the asset.

43. **What is an example of separate property that you bring into the marriage?** Here's one example:

Assume you owned a house before you were married and it was titled in your name only and that it had a fair market value of $200,000 with no mortgage—as long as it remains titled in your name only, it will be considered separate property.

Note: The payment of taxes or repairs with marital money could make it wholly or partially marital property. However, if you hired a management company to rent the house for you and all the bills were paid with rent proceeds, it could possibly still all be considered separate property.

44. **What is an example of separate property that you inherit during the marriage?** Here's one example:

Your Uncle Jim passed away and left you $20,000. As long as the money is kept in an account in your name only, it will be considered separate property.

45. **If the $20,000 inheritance from my Uncle Jim (that I have kept in a separate account) grows to $25,000, would part of that be considered marital property?** It depends on whether the growth in the account was passive or active. In other words, if you were managing the account, the $5,000 in growth may be considered marital property. However, if you have a money manager managing the account, it could still be considered separate property because you would not be actively involved.

46. **What is an example of separate property that you receive as a gift?** Here's one example:

Your father gave you a gift of $12,000 for your birthday and the check was made out to you only — not you and your spouse — and you put that money into a separate account in your name only. As long as the money is kept in an account in your name only, it will be considered separate property.

47. **If my husband put $5,000 into a savings account in his name only during the marriage, is that considered separate property?** It depends on where the money came from. If it was a gift or inheritance, possibly yes. On the other hand, if it was money earned during the marriage, it would be marital property even though it's only in his name.

48. **What happens if I use my $20,000 inheritance as a down payment on a family home for my spouse and myself?** The $20,000 is now a marital asset along with the house.

49. **What if I bring a house into the marriage that is in my name only and I add my spouses name to the title?** In that case, the house is considered marital property. You have made a *'presumptive gift'* to the marriage.

50. **How is property divided during divorce?** In many cases, divorcing couples divide their property themselves (with or without the help of professionals such as lawyers, mediators or financial professionals). However, if you are unable to reach an agreement, a final division will be made by the court and it will depend, to a large degree, on whether you live in a community or an equitable property state.

51. **How is property divided in a community property state?** In community property states, community or marital property is generally divided equally (50/50) between the spouses regardless of whose name they are in.

Community property states include Alaska, Arizona, California, Idaho, Louisiana, Nevada, New Mexico, Texas, Washington, Wisconsin and Puerto Rico. The remaining states are equitable property states.

52. **How is property divided in an equitable property state?** In an equitable property state the court *'equitably divides'* the marital property. This does not necessarily mean an equal division. The court normally considers the length of the marriage, the age, health and the conduct of the parties, as well as the occupation, skills and employment in deciding what an equitable division should be.

 The court is more likely to award more property *(and fewer debts)* to:

- The spouse who has less earning ability
- A spouse who is in poor health or has other adverse circumstances
- The spouse who has custody of minor children

53. **In a 50/50 split, do we divide each asset in half?** Not necessarily. You can split each one in half or you can each take different assets of equal value. However, if you have only one large asset, such as a house and splitting it is not possible or impractical; one spouse can take the asset and give the other spouse a property settlement note for the value of their portion of the asset.

54. **What is a property settlement note?** A property settlement note is a promise to pay the other spouse the agreed upon amount. It is used when there are not enough assets or cash for one spouse to buy out the other's interest in an asset. Together you determine the number of years, interest rate and monthly amount to be paid. The payments are considered part of the property division and not taxable income to the recipient; however, any interest received is taxable income.

Note: Property settlement notes do not survive bankruptcy so it may be wise to obtain some type of collateral to ensure the payments.

55. **As the wife, shouldn't I keep the house?** Not necessarily. There are many factors that should go into this decision. For example:

a. *Can you afford to keep the house?* Before you decide that you want the house, consider all of the costs—mortgage payments, taxes, insurance, repairs and maintenance as well as other fees—it can get expensive.

Note: Don't just guess whether you can afford the house. Complete an after-divorce income and expense worksheet to ensure that the money will be there before you make a decision. Don't get caught in the trap of electing to keep the house only to have to sell it soon after the divorce because it is too costly to maintain. *(See Appendix B for an Income and Expense Worksheet.)*

b. *Examine your motives for wanting to keep the house.* Is it for kids — to provide them with a stable environment? Is it to maintain your image? Is it for sentimental value or something totally different? Consider what you gain and what you must give up to keep the house.

c. *Are there other assets that would be more beneficial to you?* Consider your goals for your future. If the house represents your portion of the assets while your husband gets investments or other liquid assets, will keeping the house really help you build a solid foundation for your new life?

56. If my spouse gets the house, what do I get?

Generally, if one spouse gets the house, the other spouse gets another asset based on the equity in the house. For example, if there is $40,000 worth of equity in the house and you are splitting assets 50/50, then you should get another asset worth $40,000. If there isn't another asset worth $40,000 an equity loan or a *property settlement note* could be drawn up so that both spouses end up with assets of equal value.

57. How do we determine the amount of equity in our home?

To determine the amount of equity in your home, enlist the aid of a realtor or professional real estate appraiser to determine the market value of your house *(the amount you could reasonably sell it for)*. Then subtract what you owe from the market value to determine the amount of equity you have.

For example, if the fair market value of your house is $200,000 and you owe $160,000 on your mortgage then the equity in your home is $40,000 [$200,000−$160,000].

58. **If my spouse gets the house, who gets the mortgage?** The mortgage generally stays with the house. So, if your spouse gets the house and your name is on the mortgage, make it a settlement condition that your spouse refinance or get a new mortgage in his/her name only. And, the same holds true for any asset that has a loan attached to it, such as cars or vacation homes, etc. As long as your name is on the loan, creditors can come after you if your ex-spouse does not pay the bill.

59. **Can we sell the house and split the proceeds?** Yes. This is always an option. However, since there are no guarantees about how long it will take to sell your house, start the process as soon as possible.

60. **How do we determine the value of household items like furniture and appliances?** Use the fair market value or the amount you could reasonably sell it for at a garage sale or a second hand store.

61. **My spouse and I have a lot of stuff. Is there a simple way to divide it?** Here's a suggestion: Divide your assets and debts into categories like rooms or types. Then take turns choosing categories until they are all gone. For example, you may end up with the living room furniture and the Visa debt while your spouse gets the family room furniture and the MasterCard debt, etc.

62. **Can we just split up our investments up based on their face value?** No. This would be a mistake. There are many differences between investments and not understanding the differences could cost you. For instance, different investments are subject to different tax treatments. Also, there may other factors that can affect their value such as loans or collateral liens, etc.

For example, savings accounts have already been taxed, while 401(k)s have not, therefore, unlike savings, when you take money out of a 401(k) or a retirement account, you may owe taxes on the entire amount. And, if you under age 59-1/2, you may also be subject to a 10 percent penalty. The combination of taxes and penalties could significantly lower the final amount you will receive from the 401(k) even though the face amount of the two accounts may be the same.

This just one example, there are numerous other differences you should be aware of so do your homework. Learn about your investments or seek advice from a financial professional so you can make informed decisions when it comes to dividing your investments.

63. **How can I learn more about the investments my spouse and I own?** Start by reading your investment account statements. If you need help, ask for it. Most financial institutions have good customer service departments. Find out who the account representative is and contact them. Read books, visit money sites on the web, attend seminars and ask questions. Remember, it's your money and your future.

64. **My spouse and I have two stocks each worth $25,000. Can I assume they represent the same value and we each take one?** Not necessarily. It depends upon what you originally paid for each one. For example, if you originally paid $10,000 for Stock A, you will owe taxes on a gain of $15,000 [$25,000 — $10,000] when you sell it.

On the other hand, if you originally paid $20,000 for Stock B, when you sell it, you will only owe taxes on a gain of $5,000 [$25,000 — $20,000]. Therefore, the stock you paid the most for (Stock B) will be worth more because your tax bill will be less. To keep the division fair, consider splitting your investments down the middle or working with a financial professional to assist you in calculating the after-tax value of each investment so you can make informed decisions.

65. **Is life insurance an asset?** It can be, if it has a cash value component. For example, whole life and universal life policies may have cash value, but term life insurance policies do not.

Note: While term life insurance is not considered an asset, it may be valuable to you especially in situations where you may be receiving payments from your ex-spouse and he can no longer qualify for a new insurance policy for health or other reasons. So, be sure that the policy stays in force as long as it is needed.

66. **What are career assets and should they be considered a part of our marital assets?** Career assets are advantages that a spouse has because of advanced degrees, their earning ability, or benefits and perks related to their job. If one spouse's career has taken priority over the others during the marriage, the value they received could be considered an asset and could impact the settlement process. Consult with an attorney or research how your state handles this issue.

67. **My spouse and I own a business that we both work in. How can we divide it?** Here are four possible options. You and/or your spouse can:

   a. Buyout the other's interest
   b. Continue to own it jointly
   c. Sell the business
   d. Split it so that you each own a portion of the business whether you continue to work together in it or not

Your decision will depend on several factors, including whether the business can survive without you or your spouse; how attached you are to it; whether or not the two of you can continue to work together productively after the divorce; and whether the business can be divided.

In either case, you will need to know the value the business. Consider hiring a business valuation expert for an objective appraisal.

68. **What if my spouse runs the business and I suspect that he is hiding information from me?** If you suspect that information may be missing, start to gather as much documentation as possible, including:

a. Income, balance sheet and cash flow statements for the business
b. Bank accounts, statements, checkbooks and canceled checks
c. Income tax returns (personal and business)
d. Financial reports
e. Applications for loans

69. **What if my spouse is hiding assets?** If you suspect that your spouse is hiding assets, do some investigative work on your own. Carefully review statements and records. If you feel the situation warrants it, hire a forensic accountant to uncover any hidden assets. Remember, only known assets can be divided.

Note: See Appendix G for a list of Resources including forensic accountants

70. **What happens to the debts we incurred during the marriage?** In general, you and your spouse will still be responsible for any debts you incurred. During the settlement process your debts should be divided along with your assets. Unlike bankruptcy where you may be released from your obligations to pay back debts, getting divorced does not erase your debt obligations.

71. **Will I still be able to use my credit cards after the divorce?** Only if they are in your name. If you do not have any credit established in your name, you should do so while the marriage is still in effect.

RECAP

How you divide property and debt is largely dependent on the state you live in. For example, in community property states the division is 50/50 while in equitable property states, the division varies based on several factors (see *Question 52*).

When you start the settlement process, after you determine if you live in a community or equitable property state, take steps to establish the current real value of your marital property and debts so you can make informed decisions before you sign off on the final settlement.

Watch Video Message: Patricia Stallworth - Chapter 4 Intro

www.psworth.com/divorcechapters

CHAPTER 4

PENSIONS AND RETIREMENT PLANS

"There comes a day when you realize that turning the page is the best feeling in the world because you realize there is so much more to the book than the page you were stuck on." — Zayn Malik

Retirement plans and pensions are sometimes your most valuable assets. It's important to understand how they work and their current worth so they can be accurately represented during the settlement process.

Chapter 4 focuses on the basics of pensions and retirement plans.

---

72. **Are pensions and retirement plans considered marital assets?** Yes.

73. **How do I find out what a pension plan is worth?** Here are three possibilities:

   a. Look for a recent pension statement that you or your spouse may have received.

Chapter 4: Pensions and Retirement Plans

    b. Contact the employer or their plan administrator and ask for the present value of the pension plan.

    c. Ask a CPA or financial professional to prepare a pension valuation.

74. What does it mean if the employer or their plan administrator just gives me a monthly amount that my husband will receive when he retires and not a present value? It means that your husband has a defined benefit plan and that he will collect a specific amount each month from his employer when he retires.

75. What is a defined benefit plan? A defined benefit plan is a type of pension plan where the employer promises to pay a specified amount when an employee retires. The amount is generally calculated using a formula based on the employee's earnings history, the amount of time they were employed with the company and their age at retirement.

76. How do I find out what a future defined benefit plan is worth now as a marital asset? You can either ask the employer or their plan administrator for the present value, or ask a CPA or financial professional to calculate the present value.

77. What if my ex-husband dies before he is eligible to receive the monthly benefit? As a part of your research, be sure you understand how each plan works. In some cases, survivor benefits can be set up before retirement — even for an ex-spouse. However, in other cases, the pension will disappear and there will be no payout.

Note: Dividing pensions is not always easy and, to complicate matters further, there are some pensions that cannot be divided. Once you understand the specifics of your case, you can make an informed decision about whether it is more advantageous for you to fight for a portion of the pension or elect to take another asset of equal value, especially if retirement is far into the future.

78. **What is a QDRO?** A QDRO is a Qualified Domestic Relations Order. It is used to divide pensions and retirement plans and transfer the funds without incurring taxes.

79. **How does a QDRO work?** Here are two examples:

Example 1: If the retirement plan is a defined benefit plan with payments to start at the retirement of the employee, a QDRO can be used to divide the monthly payment so that each spouse receives a portion. So, if the monthly payment is $2,000 and each spouse is to get 50%, they will each get $1,000 per month. *Note:* If your spouse continues to work and gets a higher payout at retirement, $2,300 for example, the payment for the non-employee spouse will still be set at $1,000.

Example 2: If the retirement plan has cash in it like a 401(k), a QDRO can be used to divide the cash up with a portion going to each spouse. So, if there is $200,000 in the account and you get a 50/50 split — $100,000 will remain in the account and $100,000 will go to the other spouse.

80. **What should I do with money that I receive from a 401(k) split?** Here are three options:

1. You may have the option to leave your portion in a separate account in your spouse's company plan
2. You can have it transferred to an IRA in your name
3. You can take it out and spend it.

81. **What are the pros and cons of leaving money that I receive from a 401(k) split in my spouse's company plan?** If this is an option, a pro is that you don't have to do anything. The funds will simply be transferred into a separate account for you.

A con is that your investment choices may be limited. You will have to choose from the investments that the company offers and you may not be able to add any additional funds to your account.

82. **How do I get money transferred from my spouses' retirement plan to an IRA?** You will need to contact a bank, broker or investment company to set up an IRA account and request that your share or distribution be transferred directly to your IRA as a part of the QDRO.

83. **What happens if I choose to spend all or part of the money that I receive from a 401(k) split? If I'm under 59 1/2, will I have to pay a 10 percent penalty?** Money transferred as a result of a QDRO offers you a one-time opportunity to take money out without incurring a 10 percent penalty if you are under age 59 1/2. However, money you take out, that is money that you do not directly transfer into another retirement account such as an IRA, will be considered taxable income and you may have to pay taxes on it. Also, remember this is a one-time opportunity, any future withdrawals may be subject to both taxes and penalties.

84. **Is a QDRO required to divide an IRA?** No, and the same holds true for SEP-IRAs and deferred annuities. To divide these accounts, contact the managing firm or broker and complete the required paperwork for the transfer.

85. **Can I take money out of an IRA that's transferred to me and spend it without a penalty if I'm under 59 1/2 like I can with a 401(k) in *Question 83*?** No. Since you do not use a QDRO to divide an IRA, it is not subject to the same rules. If you take the money out of the IRA and spend it, and you are under 59 1/2, you will be subject to both taxes and a 10 percent penalty.

RECAP

Pensions and retirement plans can easily be the most valuable assets you own as a couple, so it's important to understand what they are, how they work and what they are worth.

Remember, not all investments are not created equal even though they may have the same face value. This is especially true with retirement accounts. The tax treatment of various retirement assets can make a big difference in the bottom line amount you receive. To avoid inequities in the division of retirement assets, don't just look at the face value. Instead, split them down the middle or calculate the after-tax value of each investment before you split them up.

Watch Video Message: Patricia Stallworth - Chapter 5 Intro

www.psworth.com/divorcechapters

CHAPTER 5

SOCIAL SECURITY

"When you change the way you look at things, the things you look at change."
— Wayne Dyer

As long as you and/or your spouse have paid into Social Security, you may be eligible for benefits. Understanding those benefits is key to making the best decisions for your future.

Chapter 5 reviews basic questions relating to Social Security benefits.

---

86. My spouse was married and divorced once before. Will I be able to receive a portion of his Social Security benefits after the divorce? Yes, as long as he is eligible to receive Social Security benefits and you meet the following requirements:

    a. You were married for at least 10 years before the divorce is final

    b. You have not remarried

    c. You are age 62 or over

d. You are not eligible to receive a Social Security benefit that equals or exceeds one-half of your former spouse's benefit.

87. **If I am eligible to receive a portion of my ex-spouses' benefits, do I have to wait until my spouse starts receiving Social Security benefits before I can start receiving mine?** No, as long as you meet the requirements outlined in *Question 86*, and you have been divorced at least two years, you can start receiving a portion of your former spouse's benefits regardless of whether he has retired or has applied for benefits.

88. **What portion of my former spouse's Social Security benefits can I expect to receive?** Generally, the most you can expect to receive is one-half of your former spouse's benefit. For example, if his monthly benefit is $800, the maximum you will receive is $400. *Note:* If you are eligible to receive benefits yourself, check to see which is greater — your full benefits or one-half of your former spouses before you sign up.

89. **If my spouse dies after the divorce, can that affect my Social Security benefits?** Yes. The death of your ex-spouse could possibly increase your benefits. You may be eligible to receive a full widow's benefits, which equals 100 percent of your former spouse's benefits, as long as your deceased spouse was eligible to receive Social Security benefits and you meet the following requirements:

a. You had been married at least 10 years before the divorce was final
b. You are age 60 or over, or you are between ages 50 and 60 and disabled

c. You have not remarried
d. You are not entitled to receive a benefit that equals or exceeds your deceased ex-spouse's benefit.

RECAP

If you are eligible for Social Security now or will be at some time in the future it's important to understand what you need to do to receive those benefits. This can be an added source of income in retirement so don't overlook it or undervalue it as a benefit.

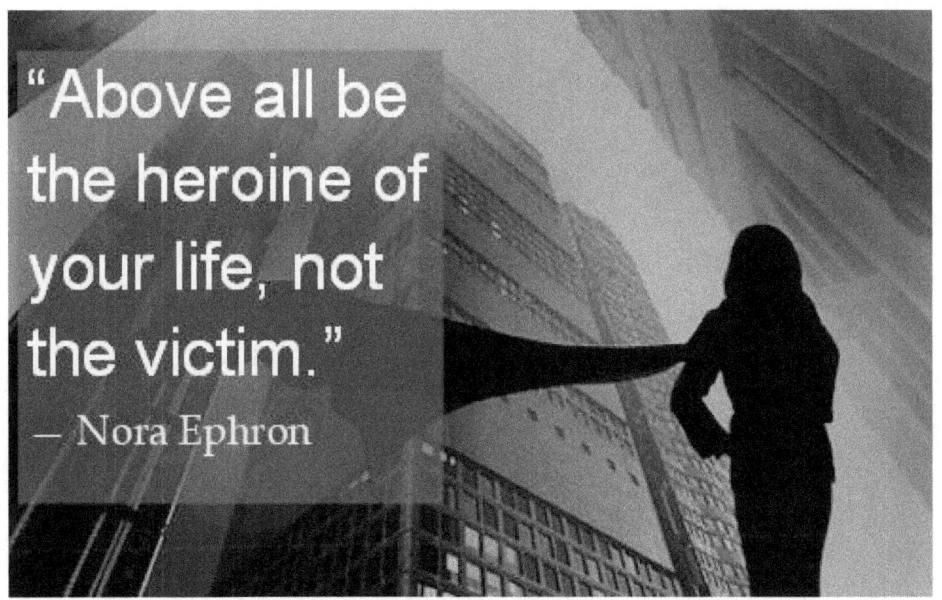

Watch Video Message: Patricia Stallworth - Chapter 6 Intro

www.psworth.com/divorcechapters

CHAPTER 6

ALIMONY

"Above all be the heroine of your life, not the victim." — Nora Ephron

According to several prominent attorneys, alimony, once a given for many women, is now becoming less of an option. With the rise of the two-income family, it seems that the courts are becoming less and less inclined to assign alimony in divorce cases. And, when they do, it's not uncommon for it to be limited to a specific time period even in long-term marriages.

Chapter 6 answers basic questions about alimony and explores alternatives to consider if alimony is not an option in your case or if it is so limited that it does not offer you much relief.

---

90. **What is alimony?** Alimony, sometimes called spousal support, maintenance, or rehabilitative support, is a series of payments from one spouse to the other after a divorce. The general purpose is to balance the differences between the earning abilities of the spouses.

Chapter 6: Alimony

91. **Will I receive alimony and if so, how much?** Whether or not you receive alimony depends on a number of factors. If you and your spouse cannot reach an agreement on your own and your case goes to court, a judge or jury might use some of the following criteria to make a decision:

- The actual need of each spouse
- The ability of your spouse to pay
- The duration of the marriage
- The age, physical and emotional health of each spouse
- The standard of living established during the marriage
- The earning capability, education and employability of each spouse.

Note: New experts called 'vocational evaluators' are emerging that assess the job and income prospects for a spouse who hasn't been fully employed outside of the home for a while. They administer vocational tests and then shop the spouse's credentials with potential employers in order to estimate how much income the spouse could earn and then reports their findings.

92. **What should I consider when determining the amount of alimony I will need?** First develop a list of your expenses. Then subtract any income you will have. The difference is the minimum amount you will need. Since alimony is taxable income, you may need to add an additional amount to the cover taxes. For example, if you will need $800 a month and you are in a 20 percent tax bracket (including Federal and state), you will actually need $1,000 per month to end up with $800 after taxes [$1,000 x 0.20 (tax bracket) = $800].

93. **What if my husband refuses to pay alimony?** If the court has ordered alimony payments and your spouse refuses to make the required payments, take immediate legal action to enforce the order through a 'contempt' proceeding or an 'earnings assignment order.' Orders to pay monthly alimony have the same force as any other court order.

94. **Are there alternatives to receiving alimony?** Yes. Consider taking more assets in exchange for alimony. This will eliminate the risk associated with waiting to receive alimony payments and continuing to tie your livelihood to your ex-spouse.

95. **Who pays the taxes on alimony?** In the past, the person who received it paid taxes on it as a part of their income and the person who paid it got to deduct it from their taxable income. However, because of recent tax law changes – that will no longer be the case. Alimony will no longer be considered taxable income or a tax deduction.

96. **Are there different types of alimony?** Yes open-ended and non-modifiable.

- Open-ended alimony is open to review. It can be increased, decreased or stopped altogether as circumstances change.

- Non-modifiable alimony is just as the name implies. It is to be paid for as long as stated in the court order without the option to modify it.

97. **What if I am awarded alimony for 6-years and my ex-spouse dies in 2-years?** That's a problem because alimony stops upon the death of the payer, so you should consider securing your payments in some way either with other assets or a life insurance policy.

98. **How can I protect my alimony payments in the event of the death of my ex-spouse?** The court order should contain provisions for life insurance to cover the life of the person paying the alimony.

Note: It is best to get the policy before the divorce is final, so that you know if your spouse can qualify for a policy and that he will cooperate in obtaining such a policy. If he does not qualify for a policy or is hesitant to apply for one, it is better to know this before you sign the final papers, so you can request additional assets in lieu of alimony.

99. **Does my husband have to pay alimony if I am living with another man?** Your husband must pay alimony as long as a court order requires him to do so. However, some orders provide that alimony will stop under these circumstances. Be sure you understand all of the stipulations in your agreement or divorce decree.

RECAP

Alimony is no longer a given, so be prepared for the fact that alimony may not be awarded in your case. And, if it is awarded, it may only be for a limited amount of time. If you will be requesting alimony, be sure to discuss the probability of success in your case of receiving alimony payments with your attorney.

If your prospects are slim, begin to focus in on other assets that may have the same financial impact as alimony so that you can get off to a good start in your new life.

Also, don't forget that you and your spouse are free to work out arrangements on your own. If you reach an agreement, be sure to make it a part of the final divorce decree, so that it can be enforced if necessary.

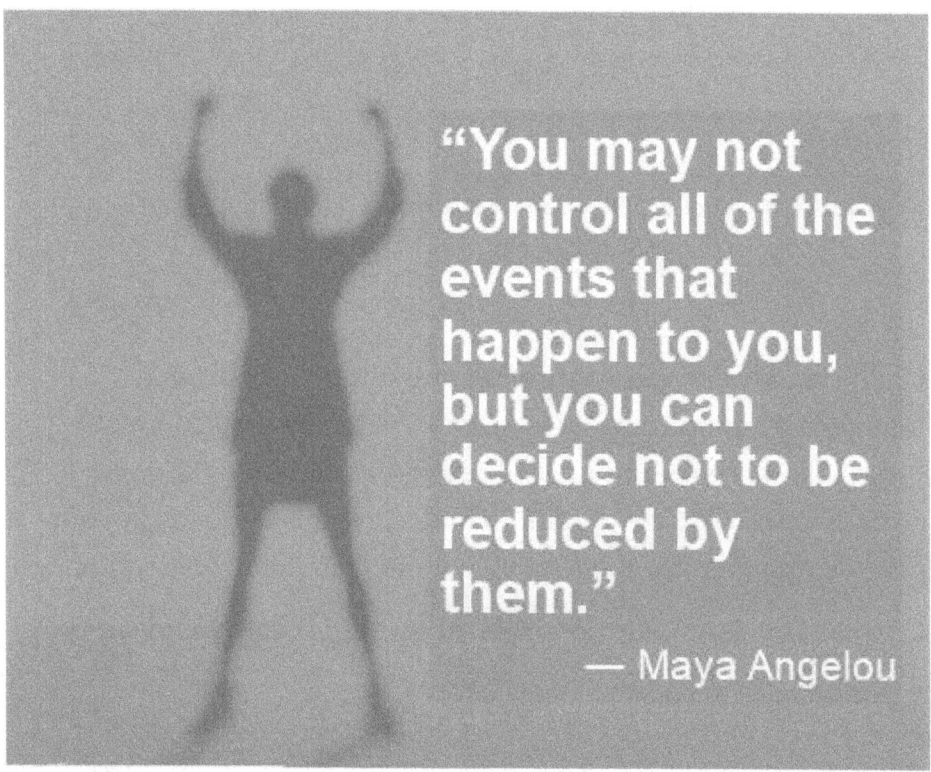

Watch Video Message: Patricia Stallworth - Chapter 7 Intro

www.psworth.com/divorcechapters

CHAPTER 7

CHILD CUSTODY AND SUPPORT

"You many not control all of the events that happen to you, but you can decide not to be reduced by them." — Maya Angelou

Child custody can raise a number of issues. The court may intervene by appointing a *guardian ad litem* who will conduct a series of interviews and make a recommendation to the court regarding the custody of minor children. If this happens in your case, be prepared for the interviews and take them very seriously.

Chapter 7 reviews questions related to child custody and support.

---

100. Do mothers automatically get custody of the children? No. the courts are most concerned with what is in the best interests of the children and they look at several factors to determine which parent is most prepared for that role.

101. What factors does the court consider during child custody cases? The primary standard is *what is in the*

best interest of the child. To arrive at this decision, the court considers a number of factors including the:

- Emotional and physical environment
- Personal safety of the children
- Moral atmosphere of the household
- Mental and physical health of the parents
- Ages of the children
- Preferences of the children
- Prior behavior of the parents
- Ability of each parent to care for the children

102. What are the main child custody options? There are three basic options:

- *Sole physical custody* – this is where one parent takes care of the child most of the time and makes major decisions about the child. That parent usually is called the *'custodial parent'* and the other parent is referred to as the *'non-custodial parent.'* The non-custodial parent almost always has a right of visitation – a right to be with the child, including overnight visits and during vacation periods.

- *Joint legal custody* – this is where both parents share in making major decisions affecting the child, such as issues related to schooling, health care, and religious training.

- *Joint physical custody* - refers to the time the child spends with each parent. The length of time could be relatively moderate, such as every other weekend with one parent; or the amount of time could be equally divided between the parents.

103. **Can a custody order be changed?** Yes. However, once a parent is awarded custody in a court order, the judge can only change it if there is a substantial change in the circumstances that could have a direct and adverse effect on the child.

104. **How do we figure out how much child support will I receive/pay and for how long?** Each state has child support guidelines or formulas that can be used to calculate the minimum amount you will receive/pay. These guidelines take into consideration things like the gross earnings of each spouse, the expenses they are currently paying for the child, how much time each child spends with the parent, etc.

In most cases, you will receive/pay child support until your child reaches the age of majority in your state, which is usually between the ages of 18 and 21. However, spouses should also consider how to handle special circumstances, such as children with disabilities.

105. **Who pays college costs?** While child support guidelines generally do not extend beyond high school, college costs should be considered. Any agreements reached between you and your spouse should be added to the final settlement.

106. **What if I need more child support in the future?** If child support is mandated by a court order, you can petition the court to increase it if you can show that there has been a substantial change in circumstances such as increased living expenses, inflation or an increase in the earnings of the other parent.

107. **If my spouse does not pay child support, do I still have to let him see the kids?** Yes. Every parent has a right to have parenting time (time to spend with their children) even if they don't pay child support as ordered by the court. Visitation, also known as parenting time, is not tied to whether or not your ex-spouse pays the child support he is supposed to pay. That is a totally separate matter.

108. **Can child support be reduced?** Yes, if there is a substantial change in the circumstances of the payer such as a job loss or a reduction in salary. In this case, the person paying child support could petition the court to decrease child support payments.

RECAP

Issues of child custody and support can get complicated. Whether you decide to work with an attorney or tackle this on your own, most states will have guidelines that you can follow. If you and your spouse work out arrangements, be sure to put them in writing so they can be part of the final divorce decree. And, remember, the courts are most concerned with the best interests of the child and they may intervene if they feel your arrangements do not reflect this.

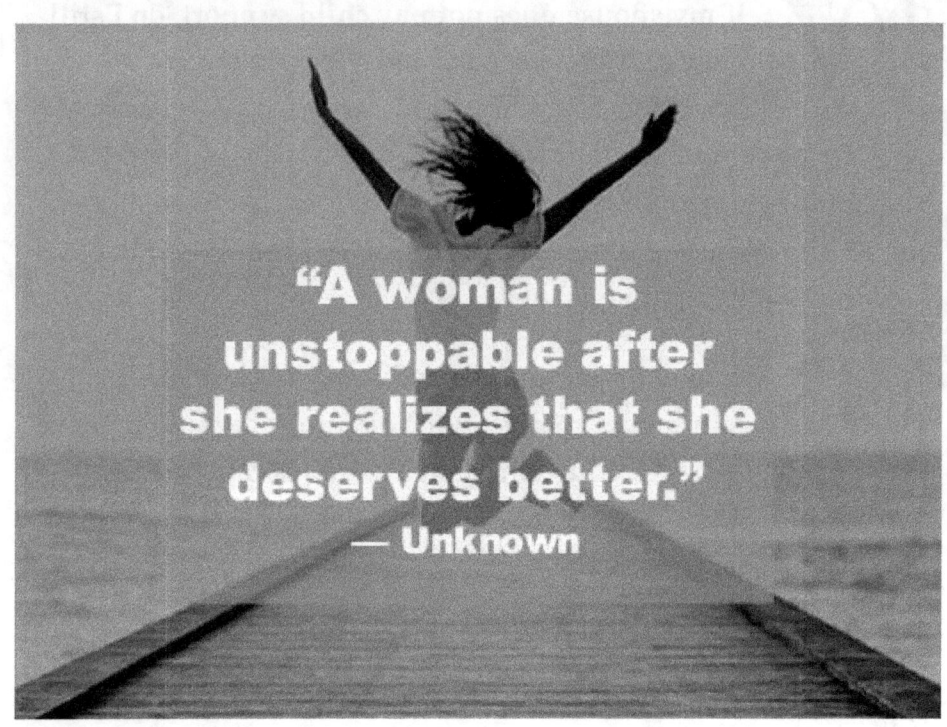

Watch Video Message: Patricia Stallworth - Chapter 8 Intro

www.psworth.com/divorcechapters

CHAPTER 8

INSURANCE AND TAXES

"A woman is unstoppable after she realizes that she deserves better." — Unknown

In the heat of divorce, insurance and taxes may be overlooked or not given the attention they deserve, but the decisions you make regarding them (or don't make) can be important to your future financial security.

Chapter 8 explores situations and discussion points regarding insurance and taxes.

109. My health insurance plan is through my spouse's company. What happens to my health coverage after the divorce? In most cases, you will be responsible for obtaining your own coverage after the divorce. Here are three basic options:

1. Continue coverage through your spouse's company with COBRA. If it is available, you can obtain sign up information from your spouse's employer.

2. Purchase a separate policy for yourself
3. If you are employed and your employer offers coverage, you can sign up there

Note: If you have children and they are covered by your ex-spouse's company policy, their coverage can stay in place even if you have custody of the children.

110. **What is COBRA?** The Consolidated Omnibus Budget Reconciliation Act (COBRA) requires companies with 20+ employees to allow ex-spouses to apply for their health insurance in their own name for three years.

Note: COBRA can be very expensive so look at other options as well.

111. **Will my ex-spouse pay the premium?** Only if it is in the court order. Normally, you will be responsible for paying the premium for your policy.

112. **Is it a good idea to have life insurance on my former spouse?** Yes, especially if you will be receiving alimony and/or child support payments because if ex-spouse dies or becomes disabled, the payments could stop. Therefore, you may also want to consider requesting disability insurance as well as life insurance to protect your payments.

Note: Always request that any policies be purchased before the divorce is final to ensure that your spouse is insurable and that he will cooperate in obtaining the policy. If your spouse is uninsurable or unwilling to obtain the appropriate coverage,

Chapter 8: Insurance and Taxes

consider requesting another asset to serve as collateral, such as a retirement account.

113. **If life insurance is purchased to protect alimony payments, who should be the owner?** If you will be receiving alimony payments, you should be the owner as well as the beneficiary to ensure that the policy stays in force.

114. **Are alimony payments taxable/deductible?** Yes, in the past, alimony was considered taxable income of the spouse who received it and a deductible expense of the spouse who paid it, as long as it met IRS guidelines. This meant that any alimony payments you received would be reduced by the amount of taxes you owed. However, on January 1, 2019 that will all change. The new tax law has eliminated the need to include alimony as income if you receive it and as a possible tax deduction if you pay it.

115. **In joint custody cases, who can claim the children as dependents?** Generally, the custodial parent *(the parent that the children spend the majority of time with)* claims them as dependents. However, since the new tax law of 2017 eliminated the use of exemptions for dependents this no longer a relevant issue in terms of tax deductions.

116. **Is child support taxable/deductible?** No. Child support is not considered taxable income nor is it deductible.

117. **April 15th will come before our divorce is final can my spouse and I file a joint tax return?** Yes, you can file a joint tax return as long as you were still married on December 31st of the prior year. If, however, you are uncomfortable filing a joint tax return, another option is to file as *married filing separately*.

118. **What is my filing status after my divorce?** Your options are to file as single or possibly head of household if you meet the eligibility requirements.

RECAP

Insurance and taxes are two of the most neglected areas when it comes to divorce planning, but they can each have a huge impact on your life after your divorce. Be sure you have appropriate insurances in place and that you understand the value of tax exemptions if you are a parent when negotiating a settlement.

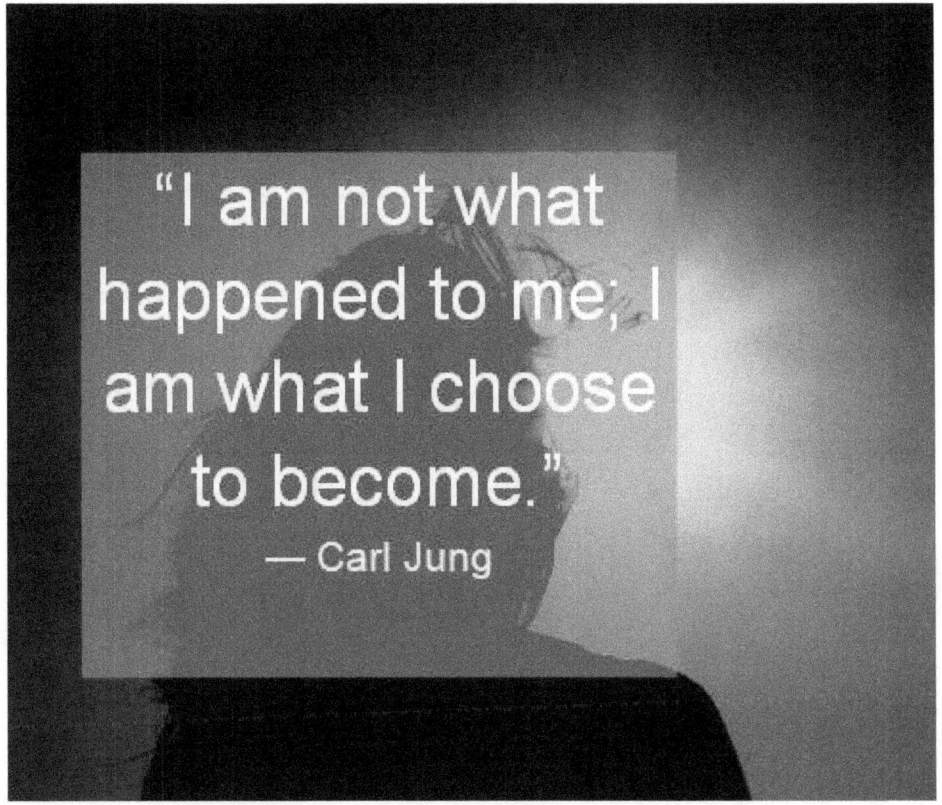

Watch Video Message: Patricia Stallworth - Chapter 9 Intro

www.psworth.com/divorcechapters

CHAPTER 9

CHOOSING AN ATTORNEY

"I am not what happened to me; I am what I choose to become." — Carl Jung

Choosing an attorney can be one of the most important decisions you make during your divorce. It can mean the difference between a bad settlement, a so-so settlement and one that gets you off to a good start in your new life. Because this can be such an emotional time, you really need to choose someone who is well versed in family law and who understands the issues you may be facing so they can be a real advocate for you.

Chapter 9 answers questions related to hiring an attorney to make the process smoother and help you achieve the best outcome.

---

119. Do I have to have an attorney? No. But unless you have no assets and no children, always consider getting legal advice. And, if any of the following circumstances apply to your situation, really consider legal representation:

- Your spouse has already hired an attorney and begun the process

- You have young children
- You and your spouse have considerable or complicated property or debt
- Your safety, or that of your children is at risk from your spouse
- You or your spouse own a business
- Your spouse is more knowledgeable about financial matters
- You are unable or unwilling to stand up for your rights
- You don't trust your spouse to be open, fair and honest
- You and your spouse are not able to communicate effectively

120. **How do I find an attorney?** This could take some work on your part. Here are some suggestions to get started:

- Ask friends who have gone through a divorce
- Ask a member of the clergy
- Visit the courthouse and observe the attorneys in action. *Note:* A phone call to the clerk's office can get you the date and location of cases and hearings.
- Contact the American Academy of Matrimonial Lawyers. *(see Appendix G)*
- Call your state and/or local bar association and ask if they have a referral service for 'family law attorneys.' *(see Appendix G)*
- Look up 'family law attorneys' in your area on the internet.

Read their bios and look for those who specialize or have experience in the areas of most concern to you such as child custody or court trials.

121. **There are so many choices. How should I select an attorney?** The best way to find out if someone is a good fit for you is to do your research and then conduct personal interviews with your top three to five choices. Finally, choose the one you feel most comfortable with in terms of expertise and their willingness to work with you. During the interviews, be prepared to explain your situation and to ask questions.

Here are some examples:

- Ask about their experience working with cases like yours, what results they feel you can reasonably expect, and how they will achieve those results. Walk away from those who promise you the moon because there are no guarantees when it comes to divorce.

- Ask specific questions about fees and services, so that you will have a good idea of how you will be billed and what costs to expect, including retainers, court costs, expert witness fees, and other expenses. Also, ask what you can do to keep the costs down.

After each interview, make a note of your feelings regarding his/her competence, interest in your case, and whether you feel this is a person you trust and can work with.

122. **Are there things I shouldn't do when choosing an attorney?** Yes. Here are three suggestions:

Chapter 9: Choosing an Attorney

1. Don't use an attorney that is a family friend or business associate of your spouse.
2. Don't use your spouse's lawyer.
3. Don't choose an attorney simply because they quoted you the lowest price.

123. What's collaborative law and should I consider it? Collaborative law is a process where attorneys, specially trained in dispute resolution, work with you and your spouse to develop a final settlement agreement through negotiation. These attorneys often use a team approach by bringing in other professionals, such as financial specialists and family therapists. The goal is to develop a settlement that represents a win-win for both sides without a court trial.

However, collaborative law is not for everyone and the process is only as effective as the team you are working with. As with any legal situation, do your due diligence before deciding to participate in the collaborative process. Also, if you fail to reach an agreement, both attorneys must withdraw and each spouse must start again with a new attorney.

124. What should I prepare to get the most out the first meeting with an attorney? It is often helpful to bring a written account of items like the following:

a. Information about your family, including the names and the ages of both you and your spouse, when and where you were married, the names and ages of any children and how long you have lived in the county and state.

b. Estimates of you family's finances such as income, expenses, property, investments, etc.

c. A statement about why you are there and what you would like help with.

Note: Appendix C contains a listing of the types of information you will need to gather for your attorney.)

125. What if I can't afford to hire a good attorney because my husband manages the money? Many women drop the ball here because they feel they cannot afford to pay for good representation. But the truth of the matter is that divorce can impact your life for many years to come and the decision to go it alone may not work in your favor. Also, if money is available in the marriage pot, most attorneys will take your case and contact your spouse's attorney or the court to include provisions so that he/she will get paid.

On the other hand, if cost really is an issue, then look for free or low cost options like Legal Aid and then do your homework. Read about all of the relevant topics discussed in this book and try to at least get someone to review your documents before you sign them.

126. Are there ways that I can save money when working with an attorney? This will depend on the attorney you choose but here are some suggestions:

- Most attorneys charge by the hour, so have a purpose in mind before you make a call or schedule a meeting with them. Write down your questions/thoughts so that you can get to the point quickly. The key is not to waste your time or theirs because the clock is ticking.

- Gather the information that your attorney requests in a timely manner. They will charge you extra if they have to do legwork for you.

- Take your time and choose an attorney that you feel comfortable with. They have a chunk of your future in their hands and they need to be there for you. If it's not working, talk with them and if that doesn't help, consider making a change. Remember, they work for you — you have the power — and having a real advocate is especially important in this situation.

RECAP

While this chapter focused on questions related to choosing an attorney, there may also be other professionals who might be helpful to your case. Use some of the same methods outlined here to find and choose the ones you want to work with. Some other professionals to consider include financial professionals — CDFAs (Certified Divorce Financial Analysts), financial planners, CPA's and divorce coaches — as well as a variety of others. I have included general contact information for additional resources in Appendix G.

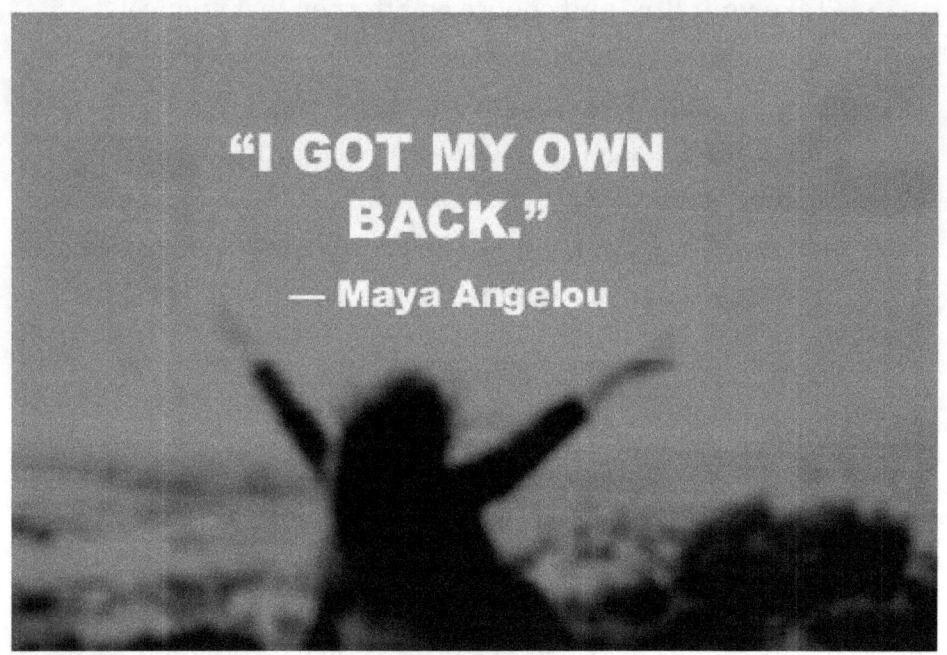

Watch Video Message: Patricia Stallworth - Planning 101

www.psworth.com/divorcechapters

EPILOGUE

PERSONAL DIVORCE PLANNING 101

"I got my own back." — Maya Angelou

Up until this point, I have covered the mechanics or the physical process you go through to get a divorce, but there is another side — the personal side. Divorce can be an emotionally charged event and it can be traumatic. But, there is also a bigger picture to be aware of and it starts as soon as the decision to get a divorce is made. That is, building a life for yourself after your divorce. To accomplish this you will need money, resources and a certain level of determination and discipline. The outcome of your divorce may determine how far you get and how quickly you get there. So, it is important, to stay focused on your goals.

One of the most difficult lessons I learned (unfortunately, I learned it after my divorce) is that...***Divorce is not about love, hate, revenge or any other emotion. Divorce is a business transaction and that means it's ultimately about money.***

Understanding the basics will give you the information you need to be an active participant. Beyond that, you need to surround yourself with competent people you trust and then let them do their job. Now, that doesn't mean that you just turn your life over to them, it simply means that you listen to them, that you participate and you are a part of the decision making process because you will have to live with the outcome.

So, how do you accomplish this? Here are three final questions to help you stay grounded.

---

127. If I know that divorce is in my future, are there things I can do before we get started to make the process smoother? Yes. Here are some examples:

a. Take an inventory or create a list of things you own, including items in safe deposit boxes and storage facilities.

b. Create a list of your debts – credit cards, loans, etc. Then get a copy of your credit report from all three credit bureaus and compare their listing to the list you created. Look for errors or loans you do not recognize and make a note of any discrepancies to dispute with the credit bureau and, if necessary, discuss with your attorney.

c. Collect and organize copies of tax returns, bills, financial statements and documents such as birth certificates and Social Security cards and place them in a safe place outside of your home such as a safe deposit box.

d. Set aside cash, prepaid cards, traveler's checks, etc. for emergencies or personal use in a safe place outside of your home.

e. Establish credit in your own name. It's not unusual for

joint accounts to be closed during divorce proceedings.

f. Change the passwords on your personal accounts, including cloud services, and get a secure email from gmail.com or a private domain that you can use to communicate with your attorney and other professionals privately.

g. Pay attention and beware of your postings on social media. That is all public information.

h. Develop a list of your current income and expenses. Calculate the amount of money you will need monthly and weekly to cover your normal expenses. *(See Appendix B for a worksheet)*

i. Envision your life after your divorce. Create a *'big picture'* plan that includes your vision for your future, income sources and expected expenses. Next, develop a list of steps you need to take and items you will need for a smooth transition to your new life.

128. During my divorce, are there things that I can do to make the process go smoother? Yes, going through a divorce can be stressful and that can throw you off track. Here are some examples of things you can do to help maintain your balance:

- Pamper yourself. Treat yourself on occasion to whatever relaxes you whether it's a spa, long walks, hanging out with friends, etc.

- Acknowledge your emotions and find someone to talk to. This could be a good friend or a therapist. Sometimes just saying things out loud helps you to process your emotions better and maintain a clearer head. Also, consider meditation and breathing exercises to alleviate some of the stress.

- Check your attitude, that is, as you participate in talks and meetings be aware of your reactions. For example, are you saying *no* out of anger or are you saying *no* because you have determined that something is not in your best interest.

- Stay focused on your *'big picture'* plan. Establish goals for how you want the process to go and the outcome you want. Then focus on those daily to help you stay on track.

- Finally, don't neglect your health. Eat right, get plenty of rest and exercise.

129. Are there things that I can do after my divorce to make things go smoother? Absolutely. Here are some examples of things you can do after your divorce to get off to a good start:

- Read your divorce papers carefully or have your attorney prepare a list of items you need to follow up on such as transferring assets, changing beneficiaries on insurance and retirement accounts, refinancing property and insuring that any necessary payments are made for insurance, etc.

    Note: Actually do the things on your follow up list. Failing to do so could not only haunt you for years and create havoc in your new life, but it could keep you unnecessarily tied to the past.

- Start to live your life on your terms. Remember, your divorce is your past and the type of future you create is up to you. Clinging to the past doesn't help anyone… least of all you. If you find yourself stuck here, find someone to talk to. It's one of the most important things you can do for your future good.

A Personal Observation

Choosing the right people to work for you is so important. I remember sitting in on a divorce case. The husband had hired a high-powered attorney and he was poised to come out a winner. It was clear that they had drawn a line in the sand and they were determined to give the wife the least amount possible. The wife, on the other hand, had hired a meek looking attorney who spoke rather softly and I remember thinking, "she's toast." But then something extraordinary happened. Each time the husband's attorney put their bottom line offer on the table for an asset, if the offer wasn't what the wife wanted, her attorney would politely say "NO" and he stood his ground until they agreed to his terms. This went on for several hours and it was fascinating to watch as the husband and his attorney slowly gave into the wife and her attorney just to end it all.

Observation takeaways: (1) she knew what she wanted; (2) she trusted her attorney to do his job and she didn't lose her cool when things got antagonistic; and (3) she chose well — she chose someone willing to fight for her. And, that's what you want — someone you can trust, someone who will help you create a plan so that you know what you want and why. You deserve no less than someone who will stand up for you — someone who really has your back!

RECAP

There are two sides to divorce — the process you go through and the personal side. The personal side is extremely important so don't ignore it because it can have a huge impact on not just the outcome of your divorce but also your life for many years.

Wishing you peace, power and prosperity! ps!

Watch Video Message: Patricia Stallworth - Workbook Overview

www.psworth.com/divorceworkbook

APPENDIX A: THE WORKBOOK - WORKSHEETS & CHECKLISTS

PREPARING FOR DIVORCE	78
PRE-DIVORCE CHECKLIST	83
DO'S & DON'T'S DURING YOUR DIVORCE	86
MASTER LIST OF INFORMATION TO COMPILE FOR YOUR DIVORCE	90
MY PRIORITIES WORKSHEET	95
INTERVIEWING & WORKING WITH LAWYERS	97
CHECKLIST OF ITEMS TO PREPARE FOR LAWYER INTERVIEWS	99
LAWYER INTERVIEW CHECKLIST	101
CHECKLIST OF ISSUES TO DISCUSS WITH YOUR LAWYER	105
INTTERVIEWING & WORKING WITH MEDIATORS	107
CHECKLIST OF ITEMS TO PREPARE FOR MEDIATOR INTERVIEWS	111
MEDIATION INTERVIEW CHECKLIST	112
CHECKLIST OF ISSUES TO DISCUSS DURING MEDIATION	114
FINANCIAL WORKSHEETS	116
INCOME AND EXPENSE	117
ASSETS AND LIABILITIES	121
HOUSEHOLD INVENTORY WORKSHEET	126
BEFORE YOU SIGN THE FINAL PAPERS CHECKLIST	127
AFTER DIVORCE CHECKLIST	130

Watch Video Message: Patricia Stallworth
- Pre-Divorce

www.psworth.com/divorceworkbook

PREPARING FOR DIVORCE

Divorce is devastating under any circumstances, but if you are unprepared, it can be even more so. This section was designed to help you take some pre-divorce steps to make the process smoother and avoid some of the post-divorce pitfalls.

Note: If you have been served with divorce papers, seek legal assistance immediately. If you don't respond to a divorce petition within the specified time frame provided for by the divorce laws of your state, you could lose the ability to contest the provisions outlined in the initial papers.

If you are just considering a divorce, but have yet to take any steps, a little planning can go a long way and it allows you to begin preparing for your life.

Here are 22 pre-divorce strategies that can help during the divorce and even after everything is finalized.

1. Envision your life after your divorce. Create a *'big picture'* plan that includes your vision for your future, income sources and expected expenses. Next, develop a list of steps you need to take and items you will need for a smooth transition to your new life.

2. Start building your case by keeping a track of everything that will help your position in your divorce. This can include keeping a record of everything that you do with the children, such as taking them to the doctor, birthday parties, or anything that supports your position as a parent. If your spouse abuses you, take pictures and record dates. If your spouse gets arrested, uses drugs, or drinks to excess, make notes of anything that will back up the problem.

3. Consult an attorney early in the process. Remember, you can consult a lawyer about your options without starting the actual divorce process or committing to anything.

4. Open a checking account in your name and get a P.O. Box. This will allow you to pay your attorneys' fees and other expenses without having to worry about your husband finding out or taking the money. Have your bank statements sent to a friend's house or your P.O. Box.

5. Begin to build a cash reserve to cover emergency expenses, attorney fees, rent, deposits, utilities, etc.

6. Don't quit your job, as you will need the financial security after you divorce.

7. If you don't already have a credit card in your name, apply for one now. It's generally easier to establish credit when you are married.

8. Make sure that all federal, state, and local taxes are paid to date. If you suspect that your spouse has not reported taxes

properly and stands to be audited, consider filing amended tax returns as married-filing separately. This may cost more now but it could really save you in the end. The last thing you want after your divorce is a call from the IRS.

9. Get a safety deposit box to store valuable documents and jewelry.

10. Videotape your possessions, including the contents of your house, your vehicles, and other possessions. If things end up missing during the divorce, this can provide proof of its existence. It can also help jog your memory when it comes time to divide the marital property.

11. Change the passwords on your personal accounts, including cloud services, and get a secure email from gmail.com or a private domain that you can use to communicate with your attorney and other professionals privately. This will prevent cyber-spying by your soon-to-be ex.

12. Pay attention and beware of what you post on social media. Remember, that is all public information.

13. If you are covered on your spouse's insurance, get complete medical and dental checkups done for you and the children. Have any necessary procedures done now while you are covered. Also, start checking into getting your own coverage for health, automobile, and home, etc.

14. Have your vehicle thoroughly inspected and repaired. Having to make costly repairs or needing to buy a new car

Having to make costly repairs or needing to buy a new car can crush your budget once the divorce is finalized.

15. Even though it may be tempting to just move out of the family home, check with your lawyer first to find out what the legal implications would be. In some states, it may have an effect who gets the house and final custody decisions.

16. If you are already separated, don't start dating. This will anger your spouse and decrease your chances of getting cooperation during the divorce.

17. Don't build additional debt. If you and your husband are separated or a divorce is imminent you might consider putting a freeze on home equity credit lines and other credit accounts. Send creditors a letter by certified mail requesting that a freeze be put on joint accounts. State that you refuse to be responsible for charges made after the date of the letter. Remember, you won't be able to close the account until the balance is paid off.

18. Don't sign any documents without first consulting with a lawyer.

19. Don't neglect your health. Eat right, exercise. Acknowledge your emotions and find someone to talk to -- a good friend or a therapist.

20. Set aside time to pamper yourself. This could take some time and it will most certainly be stressful even under the best of circumstances.

21. Check your attitude, that is, as you participate in talks and meetings be aware of your reactions. For example, are you saying *no* out of anger or are you saying *no* because you have determined that something is not in your best interest.

22. Finally, stay focused on your *'big picture'* plan. Establish goals for how you want the process to go and the outcome you want. Then focus on those daily to help you stay on track.

APPENDIX A: PRE-DIVORCE CHECKLIST

The purpose of the Pre-Divorce Checklist is to help you prepare for your divorce. Complete it in as much detailed as possible.

1. Why do you want a divorce? List your top three reasons:

   _____
   _____
   _____

2. If you don't want a divorce but your spouse does, how will you move forward? List three things you can do to help you get onboard and work toward the best outcome for yourself:

   _____
   _____
   _____

3. How will your life change for the better after your divorce? *These represent your opportunities:*

   _____
   _____
   _____

4. How will your life be worse after your divorce? *These represent your areas of vulnerability:*

   _____
   _____
   _____

5. If you are a victim of domestic violence, get outside help as soon as possible. There is a national domestic abuse hotline (800-799-7233) as well as local help centers and legal aid programs available. Do not feel you have to face this alone.

   Note: If you have to move and you want custody of your kids, get legal advice first. It is generally not recommended that you move out and leave them.

6. Gather some preliminary information:
   - ❏ Make copies of important financial documents for the past three years and keep them in a safe place. *Note:* Do not take or destroy the originals. *(See Appendix C for a complete list of documents to gather.)*

   - ❏ Get a copy of your credit reports from the three major credit bureaus and make a note of any items you do not recognize. Free copies are available at www.AnnualCreditReport.com

7. Do your homework:
   - ❏ Learn about divorce including the process in your area – learn what's involved, your options and the cost. Look for programs, online classes, etc. to educate yourself.

   - ❏ Learn about managing money, especially budgeting and

credit and debt skills.

- [ ] Decide the type of divorce you want (amicable or not) then interview divorce attorneys/professionals who are experienced in achieving those outcomes. *Note: Always ask the cost for a preliminary interview – some are free but others are not.*

- [ ] Decide on some basics for your life during your divorce, such as:
    1. Where you will live?
    2. What are your expenses and how much money you will need to cover them? Where will the money come from
    3. What about the custody and care of your children?
    4. How will you pay for your divorce? Do you have the funds available or can you ask for this in the divorce settlement?

- [ ] Get your personal finances in order i.e., credit in your own name, personal savings, etc.

- [ ] Decide what's important to you and why. List your top three *must haves* in your divorce settlement :

    _____
    _____

- [ ] Decide what's important to your *spouse*. List the top three *must haves* you think he/she wants. Note: This will be important in your negotiations:

    _____
    _____

DO'S & DON'TS DURING YOUR DIVORCE

DO's

1. Do seek legal advice before you begin divorce proceedings. Remember, you can consult a lawyer about your options without starting the actual divorce process or committing to anything.

2. Do begin planning and building your new life before your divorce. At this point you need to start considering how you will handle your finances and details about your new life such as where you will live and how you will support yourself.

3. Do consider separating your personal financial life from your soon-to-be-ex before you file for divorce. In some states there is an automatic restraining order prohibiting either party from transferring, withdrawing, borrowing against, or changing the beneficiaries of any marital assets once the divorce papers are served. So for example, if you have your paycheck deposited into a joint account, consider transferring it to a new account in your name only.

4. Do ask your lawyer before closing joint accounts. In most states, you are generally entitled to half of the value of all joint accounts and your lawyer may advise you to take half of the money, and then remove your name from accounts. **But get advice first**. Doing this protects you in the event that your spouse decides to clean out the account in reaction to divorce proceedings. If you are going to withdraw half of the funds,

be sure to make a copy of the account statement showing the full balance. Then make a copy of your withdrawal slip showing the remaining balance.

5. Do make sure you have a good/current inventory of all property, owned separately or jointly in the marriage. (See the Household Inventory Worksheet and the Assets and Liabilities Worksheets)

6. Do make sure you know where all of your cash or other liquid assets are prior to filing; consult with your attorney about protecting these assets during the divorce proceedings.

7. Do make sure you know all of your current debt balances before sitting down with an attorney. (See the Assets and Liabilities Worksheets)

8. Do make sure that once you filed for divorce that all credit cards are turned off to prevent the other spouse from running them up once they learn about the divorce. *Note: If you don't have credit cards in your name only, open one before the divorce is final.*

9. Do make sure you keep contacts with your attorney or his/her assistants as brief as possible. *Ask your questions, but make every call/conversation count. In fact, you might want to make a list of questions and fax them to your attorney; this way you'll have time to make sure all of your questions are clear and it'll help you avoid multiple calls.*

DON'Ts

1. Don't try to go it alone especially if you have been in a long-term marriage or you have a lot of assets. Seek financial and legal advice. It's a good idea to consult with a CPA or divorce financial planner before you ever begin divorce proceedings. They can help advise you on strategies for dividing the marital assets, in addition to tax planning and any financial moves you need to make before the divorce is finalized.

2. Don't clean out all of your bank accounts and *hide the money* without getting proper direction from your attorney.

3. Don't use your attorney as a therapist to vent your anger and frustrations. Note: That not part of their job *(and they generally don't make good therapists)* but you'll pay the price when you get your bill at the end of the month!

4. Don't expect to be able to correspond with your attorney or their assistants via e-mail; most lawyers agree it's extremely unsafe to use this method for exchanging attorney-client privileged information. Phone or faxes are your two best options.

5. Don't agree to anything (either verbally or in writing) without getting your attorney's approval! You've hired an attorney to protect your interests… *so let them earn their pay!*

6. Don't agree to any sort of settlement without making sure that your name has been taken off any and all liabilities, or potential liabilities. This means releasing you from all joint obligations, such as mortgages, credit cards and auto leases/

loans. You must first be released either through re-financing or paying off the debts prior to signing the final agreement. Otherwise, you could find yourself chained to your soon-to-be-ex forever.

TO-DO LIST	DEADLINE	COMPLETED
1		
2		
3		
4		
5		
6		
7		
8		
9		
10		
11		
12		
13		
14		
15		
16		
17		
18		
19		
20		
21		

Watch Video Message: Patricia Stallworth
- Master List

www.psworth.com/divorceworkbook

MASTER LIST OF INFORMATION TO COMPILE FOR YOUR DIVORCE

If you will be working with an attorney and/or going through the mediation process, it is essential that you provide them with as much pertinent information as possible. Here is a checklist of some of the essential items to gather so they have a complete picture of your situation and nothing is left out of the settlement.

Note: Because of the sheer volume of information you will need to gather, consider creating a filing system with separate folders for each category so that you can access information quickly.

Information about you:

☐ Your name, address and phone number

☐ Date of birth

☐ Job title, work address and phone number

☐ Current employment and proof of income (employment contracts, W2's, 1099s, etc.)

☐ List of education/degrees/training

☐ Job history and income potential if underemployed

☐ Employee benefits statement

☐ Copies of retirement or pension plans

☐ Copies of insurance policies (life/health/disability/auto)

Information about your (cont.):

- ☐ List of separate property (property that you owned prior to the marriage or your inherited or received as a gift during the marriage)

Information about your spouse:

- ☐ Spouses' name, address and phone number
- ☐ Date of birth
- ☐ Job title, work address and phone number
- ☐ Name and address of spouses' lawyer (if applicable)
- ☐ Current employment and proof of income (employment contracts, W2's, 1099s, etc.)
- ☐ List of education/degrees/training
- ☐ Job history and income potential if underemployed
- ☐ Employee benefits statement
- ☐ Copies of retirement or pension plans
- ☐ Copies of insurance policies (life/health/disability/auto)
- ☐ List of separate property (property that your spouse owned prior to the marriage or your inherited or received as a gift during the marriage)

Marriage information:

- ☐ Date and place of marriage

Marriage information (cont.):

- ☐ Copy of marriage certificate
- ☐ Length of time you have lived in this state
- ☐ Names and dates of birth of children
- ☐ Prior marriages of you or your spouse and details of termination
- ☐ Children of prior marriages and custodial arrangements
- ☐ Copies of prenuptial agreements
- ☐ A statement of why you want a divorce
- ☐ A statement of why your spouse wants a divorce
- ☐ Date of separation / Copy of any separation agreement
- ☐ Incidences of domestic abuse or threats
- ☐ Information on any pending civil lawsuit claims where either or both spouses are listed as plaintiffs.
- ☐ Other:

  _____

Financial and tax records for you and your spouse: *(1-3 years of information)* Note: *You can use the following worksheets to help compile your information:* <u>Household Inventory Worksheet</u>; <u>Income and Expense Worksheet</u> *and the* <u>Assets and Liabilities Worksheet.</u>

- ☐ Bank statements (checking, savings, money market, CDs, etc.
- ☐ Statements on all credit cards, including current balances

Appendix A: The Workbook - Master List to Compile

Financial and tax records for you and your spouse (cont.):

- ☐ W2's / 1099s
- ☐ Tax returns for the past 3-5 years (federal, state and local)
- ☐ Applications for loans / Pending loan documents
- ☐ Retirement account statements (pensions, deferred compensation or employee benefits, stock options, 401(k), IRA, etc.) *(Note: some plans may need to valued to obtain the present day value.)*
- ☐ Investment statements (stocks, bonds, mutual funds, annuities)
- ☐ Statements for children's accounts (529, custodial college savings, etc.)
- ☐ Utility bills
- ☐ Other bills *(e.g. school tuition, unreimbursed medical bills, music lessons for children, etc.)*
- ☐ Monthly budget worksheet
- ☐ List of autos and recreational vehicles (description, loan balance, current value)
- ☐ Current market value of home and balance on for all mortgages, home equity loans or lines of credit
- ☐ Current balance on student loans
- ☐ Statements for any other private loans, verbal or written in which one or both spouses are debtor(s).
- ☐ Copy of homeowners insurance policy
- ☐ Real property appraisals

Financial and tax records for you and your spouse (cont.):

- ☐ Statement of any outstanding loans or verbal promises to repay a loan in which one or both spouses are the creditor(s).
- ☐ List of personal property (including home furnishings, jewelry, artwork, computers, home office equipment, clothing and furs, etc.) and the current value
- ☐ List of contents of safety deposit boxes / storage units, etc.
- ☐ Copies of wills / trusts
- ☐ Copies of living wills
- ☐ Copies of Powers of Attorney
- ☐ Copies of credit reports
- ☐ Copies of Advance Care Directives

Family business records:

- ☐ Name and type of business
- ☐ If you or your spouse work in the business - job title(s)
- ☐ Percent of ownership by you/your spouse
- ☐ Current value of business holding (copies of business valuations/appraisals)
- ☐ Bank statements of business
- ☐ Business tax returns (3-5 years)
- ☐ Applications for loans
- ☐ Financial statements (income, balance sheets, cash flow)

Watch Video Message: Patricia Stallworth
- Priorities

www.psworth.com/divorceworkbook

MY PRIORITIES WORKSHEET

During the settlement process, it's important to know what your priorities are so that you can fight for the items that mean the most to you and will be most helpful to you in your new life. Just saying "I want it all!" is not helpful and it might cause you to walk away with all the wrong things. So, take a moment to identify your priorities before you enter into any serious negotiations and share this information with your lawyer. Add or delete sections to fit your individual case.

Property Division

My priorities are:

a) _____

b) _____

c) _____

d) _____

My spouse's priorities are:

a) _____

b) _____

c) _____

d) _____

NOTES:

MY PRIORITIES WORKSHEET (cont.)

Finances (spousal support, division of assets and debts)

My priorities are: My spouse's priorities are:

a) _____   a) _____

b) _____   b) _____

c) _____   c) _____

d) _____   d) _____

Children (support, custody, visitation)

My priorities are: My spouse's priorities are:

a) _____   a) _____

b) _____   b) _____

c) _____   c) _____

d) _____   d) _____

NOTES:

Watch Video Message: Patricia Stallworth
- Lawyers & Mediators

www.psworth.com/divorceworkbook

INTERVIEWING & WORKING WITH LAWYERS

It is important to choose a lawyer with whom you are comfortable and who knows divorce law. So where do you find a good divorce lawyer?

Look for a lawyer who specializes in family law. This is an important step in your life and it should be handled by the most qualified legal representation that you can afford. (See Q: 120 in the book for suggestions to locate a local attorney.)

Because this is such an important decision, try to set up an initial interview with at least three attorneys before making a decision. The initial interview is usually free or relatively inexpensive (however, ask before you set the appointment), but it will give you a good overview of what you will be facing.

It is important to note that as you go through the initial interview and discuss your case with a lawyer, he or she will not then be able to subsequently represent your spouse. This is definitely something to keep in mind when you are starting a divorce.

When interviewing a lawyer, it helps to look at it as if it is a job interview and you are the employer (which in essence you are).

Ask prospective lawyers how they will proceed with your case, what would be a fair settlement, and how much it will cost. As you go through the interview, ask yourself whether this is someone who seems to understand your situation and if you are comfortable with how they suggest handling your case.

Note: If your husband has filed in a different town or state, you might consider interviewing lawyers that practice in that district. This is because local lawyers are familiar with the area's court systems and judges, and are familiar with the other lawyers that practice family law.

Once you have narrowed down your search, your interviews will give you some insight into who will best represent you. It's important to remember that a lawyer can help guide you and suggest strategies, but you are the one who ultimately calls the shots. So, take your time and choose a lawyer that you feel comfortable working with so that it can be a team effort.

Be prepared and ask the right questions when interviewing lawyers so you can choose the best fit for your case. First assemble the items on the <u>Checklist of Items to Prepare for Lawyer Interviews.</u> Then take the <u>Lawyer Interview Checklist</u> with you as you interview prospective attorneys and be sure to make a note of their answers.

Once you have an attorney, use the <u>Checklist of Issues to Discuss with Your Lawyer</u> to be sure to be sure all of your concerns get addressed.

CHECKLIST OF ITEMS TO PREPARE FOR LAWYER INTERVIEWS

Interviewing lawyers is important to find out if they are a good fit for you and your situation. However, do not come to the meeting empty handed. Here are some basics to bring or be prepared to discuss during your attorney interview meetings:

Information about you and your spouse:

☐ Your name, address and phone number

☐ Date of birth

☐ Current employment/job title/ work address and phone number

☐ Current income

☐ Name and address of spouse's lawyer (if applicable)

Marriage information:

☐ Date and place of marriage

☐ Names and dates of birth of children

☐ Prior marriages of you or your spouse and details of termination

☐ Children of prior marriages and custodial arrangements

☐ Length of time you have lived in this state

Marriage information (cont.):

☐ Why you want a divorce / why your spouse wants a divorce

☐ Approximate value of assets

☐ Approximate value of debts

Information about a family business:

☐ Type of business / Number of years in business

☐ Percent of ownership by you/your spouse

☐ Current income

LAWYER INTERVIEW CHECKLIST

Your attorney is most important advocate in your divorce, so choose well. Use this form to make notes during each interview to help you make an informed decision.

Attorney Name
_____

Law Firm
_____

Office Hours _____ Telephone _____

Email
_____

Address
_____

Appointment date/time _____

QUESTIONS

What percentage of your practice is family law? _____

How long have you practiced divorce law? _____

Do you know or have you ever represented my husband? _____

Who will be handling my case?
_____

How long will my case take? _____

How much will this cost? _____

What is your hourly rate? _____

How is court time charged?
_____

What is your billing schedule? _____

Do you have a retainer agreement? _____

How much is the retainer/ is it refundable?
_____

What is the best way to reach you if I have questions?
_____

What are the best times to reach you? _____

Will I be billed for phone calls and if so, how much?
_____

How quickly can I expect phone calls to be returned?
_____

When is the best time to schedule meetings?
_____

How will my case be handled if you are out of town? Whom can I contact? _____

What if I can't meet during normal business hours?
_____

Will you keep me informed on the status of my case? _____

Appendix A: The Workbook - Lawyer Interview Checklist

What is expected of me?
_____

What can I do to help in my case?
_____

Can I file for temporary maintenance, child custody, and child support? _____

Are you experienced in custody litigation/the dividing large assets/etc.? (ask about your biggest concerns)
_____

What strategies do you suggest for getting a fair settlement?
_____

Will I be able to get alimony? _____

What is your preferred method of settling disputes?
_____

Do I have a choice of courts, and does it make a difference?
_____

As soon as you leave the interview make a note of your general impressions while they are still fresh in your mind.

General Impressions:

Do you feel comfortable talking to this lawyer? _____

Does this lawyer seem optimistic about your case? _____

Is this lawyer straightforward about your situation? _____

Does the lawyer seem competent in the major areas of concern to you, i.e., child custody/dividing large assets/etc.? _____

Do you believe that this lawyer is interested in your case and will do a good job for you? If so, what makes you believe this? _____

_____

_____

NOTES:

CHECKLIST OF ISSUES TO DISCUSS WITH YOUR LAWYER

Once you select an attorney it will be important to be sure to discuss all relevant topics with him/her. Some key areas include the following:

Property Issues

- ☐ Equity in your home
- ☐ Other real property
- ☐ Home furnishings
- ☐ Business assets
- ☐ Professional practices
- ☐ Professional degrees
- ☐ Retirement benefits (pensions, IRAs, 401(k) plans)
- ☐ Motor vehicles
- ☐ Recreational vehicles
- ☐ Personal property
- ☐ Savings accounts
- ☐ Stocks, bonds, and funds
- ☐ Separate property
- ☐ Savings accounts
- ☐ Stocks, bonds, and funds
- ☐ Life insurance - cash value
- ☐ Compensation for contributions as a homemaker
- ☐ Hidden assets
- ☐ Other assets

Debts

- ☐ Joint/Marital debts
- ☐ Bankruptcy issues
- ☐ Income tax liabilities
- ☐ Attorneys fees and expenses
- ☐ Clauses to hold the other spouse harmless and indemnification in case your ex fails to live up to his/her obligations

Issues Relating to Children

- ☐ Child support
- ☐ Child custody, legal/physical
- ☐ Visitation with non-custodial parent
- ☐ Grandparent visitation
- ☐ Visitation with stepchildren
- ☐ Claiming children as dependents for income tax purposes
- ☐ Health insurance for children
- ☐ Dental/vision insurance for children
- ☐ Uninsured health care costs
- ☐ Private schools/Summer camps/College costs
- ☐ Religious upbringing of children

Spousal Support Issues

- ☐ How much? How long?
- ☐ Education or other costs to return to or enter the job market
- ☐ Continued health care coverage through COBRA
- ☐ Life/Disability insurance to protect alimony payments

Other Issues

- ☐ Domestic violence
- ☐ Order for protection
- ☐ Child abuse
- ☐ Parental kidnapping
- ☐ Care and custody of pets
- ☐ Restoration of maiden your name
- ☐ Post-divorce nonfinancial support
- ☐ Events for changes in alimony/child support

INTERVIEWING & WORKING WITH MEDIATORS

Mediation is a settlement process where a neutral third party assists spouses in reaching an agreement.

The role of the mediator is to facilitate or assist communication between spouses and to offer suggestions. Mediators do not make decisions, and they do not give legal advice. When choosing a mediator, select someone who is skilled in the major issues you need to resolve, such as child custody or the division of large assets.

Mediation is most effective when spouses are able to talk with each other and they are each able to stand up for their own rights. This process may be conducted with or without the use of attorneys. However, if you have an attorney, it is a good idea to have him/her review any agreements before you sign them. Decisions made during mediation are not final unless you sign off on them.

As with an attorney, use care in selecting a mediator as this could result in your final settlement. Try to get referrals and interview at least three mediators before making a decision. FYI - always ask if there is a fee for the initial consultation so you don't get any unwanted surprises.

Also, it's important to note that working with a mediator can be less expensive than court cases but it really only works when you are willing to participate fully and that means asking questions and voicing your opposition to offers that do not work for you.

Be prepared and ask the right questions when interviewing mediators so you can choose the best fit for your case. First assemble the items on the <u>Checklist of Items to Prepare for Mediator Interviews.</u> Then take the <u>Mediator Interview Checklist</u> with you as you interview prospective mediators and be sure to make a note of their answers.

Once you have a mediator, use the <u>Checklist of Issues to Discuss During Mediation</u> to be sure all of your concerns get addressed.

CHECKLIST OF ITEMS TO PREPARE FOR MEDIATOR INTERVIEWS

Interviewing mediators is important to find out if they are a good fit for you and your situation. However, do not come to the meeting empty handed. Here are some basics to bring or be prepared to discuss during your mediator interview meetings:

Information about you and your spouse:

☐ Your name, address and phone number

☐ Date of birth

☐ Current employment/job title/ work address and phone number

☐ Current income

☐ Name and address of spouse's lawyer (if applicable)

Marriage information:

☐ Date and place of marriage

☐ Names and dates of birth of children

☐ Prior marriages of you or your spouse and details of termination

☐ Children of prior marriages and custodial arrangements

☐ Length of time you have lived in this state

☐ Any prenuptial agreements

Marriage information (cont.):

☐ Why you want a divorce / why your spouse wants a divorce

☐ Approximate value of assets

☐ Approximate value of debts

Information about a family business:

☐ Type of business / Number of years in business

☐ Percent of ownership by you/your spouse

☐ Current income

MEDIATOR INTERVIEW CHECKLIST

Using mediation to settle your divorce can be cost effective and you can get results quicker. However, it is important to choose the right mediator for your situation. Try to interview at least three mediators before making a decision and use this form to make notes.

Mediator Name
_____

Company
_____

Office Hours _____ Telephone _____

Email
_____

Address
_____

Appointment date/time _____

QUESTIONS

What training have you had? *(Note: Basic divorce mediation training is 40 hours.)*
_____

What do you cover in mediation? _____
_____

What are your fees and what do they include? _____

_____

How long have you been practicing?
_____

How long will the mediation take?
_____

How much experience do you have in successful divorce mediations? What percentage of your mediations end with a settlement?
_____

Will you provide references? *(Names of other mediators, therapists, or attorneys who vouch for your qualifications.)*
_____

_____

Do you have materials to help me and your spouse make decisions? *(A website, brochure, specific information about them, overview of divorce in your state, child support guidelines, issues to be covered in divorce mediation, relevant articles. Note: If you have the sense the materials aren't professional, so might the process be. If, on the other hand, the materials are instructive, relevant and well put together, it's more likely the mediator's process also will be.)*

_____

_____

How does he/she feel about attorney involvement? *(Note: Good mediators recommend that attorneys for both parties review the agreement, a Memorandum of Understanding. This assures you protection from any legal oversights. Mediators frequently can supply clients with a list of mediation friendly attorneys who will protect you from those legal oversights without undermining your choice to collaboratively negotiate.)*

_____

As soon as you leave the interview make a note of your general impressions while they are still fresh in your mind.

General Impressions:

Do you feel comfortable talking to this mediator?

_____

Does the mediator seem competent in the major areas of concern to you, i.e., child custody/dividing large assets/etc.?

_____

Do you believe that the mediator is interested in your case and will do a good job for you? If so, what makes you believe this?

_____

_____

CHECKLIST OF ISSUES TO DISCUSS DURING MEDIATION

Once you select an attorney it will be important to be sure to discuss all relevant topics with him/her. Some key areas include the following:

Property Issues

- ☐ Equity in your home
- ☐ Other real property
- ☐ Home furnishings
- ☐ Business assets
- ☐ Professional practices
- ☐ Professional degrees
- ☐ Retirement benefits (pensions, IRAs, 401(k) plans)
- ☐ Motor vehicles
- ☐ Recreational vehicles
- ☐ Personal property
- ☐ Savings accounts
- ☐ Stocks, bonds, and funds
- ☐ Separate property
- ☐ Savings accounts
- ☐ Stocks, bonds, and funds
- ☐ Life insurance - cash value
- ☐ Compensation for contributions as a homemaker
- ☐ Hidden assets
- ☐ Other assets

Debts

- ☐ Joint/Marital debts
- ☐ Bankruptcy issues
- ☐ Income tax liabilities
- ☐ Attorneys fees and expenses
- ☐ Clauses to hold the other spouse harmless and indemnification in case your ex fails to live up to his/her obligations

Appendix A: Checklist of Issues to Discuss During Mediation

Issues Relating to Children

- ☐ Child support
- ☐ Child custody, legal/physical
- ☐ Visitation with non-custodial parent
- ☐ Grandparent visitation
- ☐ Visitation with stepchildren
- ☐ Claiming children as dependents for income tax purposes
- ☐ Health insurance for children
- ☐ Dental/vision insurance for children
- ☐ Uninsured health care costs
- ☐ Private schools/Summer camps/College costs
- ☐ Religious upbringing of children

Spousal Support Issues

- ☐ How much? How long?
- ☐ Education or other costs to return to or enter the job market
- ☐ Continued health care coverage through COBRA
- ☐ Life/Disability insurance to protect alimony payments

Other Issues

- ☐ Domestic violence
- ☐ Order for protection
- ☐ Child abuse
- ☐ Parental kidnapping
- ☐ Care and custody of pets
- ☐ Restoration of maiden your name
- ☐ Post-divorce nonfinancial support
- ☐ Events for changes in alimony/child support

Watch Video Message: Patricia Stallworth
- Financial Worksheets

www.psworth.com/divorceworkbook

FINANCIAL WORKSHEETS

Understanding your financial situation is essential to achieving the best possible settlement. This section contains:

(1) Income and Expense Worksheet – to complete this worksheet:

- Gather paystubs, checkbooks and/or bank statements, credit card statements, loan statements, etc.
- Complete the info for each spouse
- Use your best guess to determine what your income and expenses will be after the divorce. If you are currently employed and don't expect anything to change then the number may be the same in both the 'Wife' and 'Wife After Divorce' columns. However, if you are not currently employed or you expect to move, do some research to determine how that might change after your divorce.

(2) Asset & Liabilities Worksheet – to complete this worksheet:

- Gather investment and retirement statements
- Loan documents and purchase records for large items, etc.
- Insurance records

Appendix A: The Workbook - Income and Expense

(1) Income & Expense Worksheet (Budget)   Date: _____

	INCOME AND EXPENSE WORKSHEET (BUDGET)			
	INCOME			
	Gross Monhly Income			
		Husband	Wife	Wife After Divorce
	Salary			
	Overtime			
	Commissions			
	Bonus			
	Owner's Draw			
	Pension/Retirement benefits			
	Disability benefits			
	Worker's compensation			
	Social Security			
	Unemployment			
	Rental income			
	Interest income			
	Dividend income			
	Trust income			
	Annuity income			
	Business/Partnership income			
	Royalties			
	Spousal support/Alimony			
	Child support received			
	Other income (specify)			
1	TOTAL GROSS MONTHLY INCOME			
	Monthly Deductions from Income			
		Husband	Wife	Wife After Divorce
	Federal tax (based on ____ exemptions)			
	State tax (based on ____ exemptions)			
	FICA (Social Security)			
	Medicare tax			
	Union dues			
	Health care premiums			
	Child support/alimony of a prior marriage			
2	TOTAL MONTHLY DEDUCTIONS			
3	NET MONTHLY INCOME			
	(subtract line 2 from line 1)			

	Husband	Wife	Wife After Divorce
INCOME (cont)			
Optional Monthly Deductions			
Retirement/401(k) contributions			
Deferred compensation contributions			
other items deducted from paycheck (specify)			
4 TOTAL OPTIONAL DEDUCTIONS			
5 NET AVAILABLE MONTHLY CASH			
(subtract line 4 from line 3)			
EXPENSES			
Household Expenses			
	Husband	Wife	Wife After Divorce
Mortgage/Rent			
Home equity payment			
Real estate taxes			
HOA fees			
Homeowners/Renters insurance			
Heat/Gas			
Electricity			
Telephone (including cell phones)			
Water/Sewer			
Garbage			
Laundry/dry cleaning			
Maid/Cleaning service			
Home repairs and maintenance			
Lawn/Garden			
Food (groceries, household supplies, etc.)			
Liquor, beer wine, etc.			
Cable/TV services			
Internet			
Pet care			
Other (specify)			
6 SUBTOTAL HOUSEHOLD EXPENSES			
Transportation Expenses			
Car payments			
Repairs and maintenance			
Insurance			
License			
Gas			
Alternative Transportation (trains, bus, etc.)			

Appendix A: The Workbook - Income and Expense

		Husband	Wife	Wife After Divorce
	TRANSPORTATION EXPENSES (cont)			
	Parking			
	Other (specify)			
7	SUBTOTAL TRANSPORTATION EXPENSES			
		Husband	Wife	Wife After Divorce
	Personal Expenses			
	Clothing			
	Grooming/Hair care			
	Medical (unreimbursed expenses)			
	Doctor			
	Dentist			
	Optical			
	Medication			
	Therapy			
	Life insurance			
	Other (specify)			
8	SUBTOTAL PERSONAL EXPENSES			
		Husband	Wife	Wife After Divorce
	Miscellaneous Expenses			
	Clubs/Social entertainment			
	Dining Out			
	Newspapers, magazines, books			
	Donations, church or religious			
	Vacations (cost for just you - not kids)			
	Computer/Supplies/Software			
	Other (specify)			
9	SUBTOTAL MISCELLANEOUS EXPENSES			
	Children's Expenses			
	Clothing			
	Grooming			
	Education			
	Tuition			
	Books/Fees			
	Lunches			
	Transportation			
	School-sponsored activities			
	Medical (unreimbursed expenses)			
	Doctor			
	Dentist			

CHILDREN'S EXPENSES (cont)	Husband	Wife	Wife After Divorce
Optical			
Medication			
Therapy			
Allowance			
Child care/Pre-school/After-school			
Babysitters			
Lessons/extracurricular activities/supplies			
Clubs/Summer camps			
Vacations (children only)			
Other activities			
Entertainment			
Gifts to others			
Other (specify)			
10 SUBTOTAL CHILDREN'S EXPENSES			
Credit Cards/Loans/Debts *(list credit card and loan payments not already listed)*			
	Husband	Wife	Wife After Divorce
11 SUBTOTAL CREDIT CARDS/LOANS/DEBTS			
12 NET MONTHLY INCOME *(line 3)*			
13 TOTAL MONTHLY LIVING EXPENSES			
(add lines 6-11)			
14 TOTAL MONTHLY INCOME AVAILABLE			
(line 12 minus line 13)			

Appendix A: The Workbook - Assets and Liabilities

(2) Assets & Liabilities Worksheet   Date: _____

ASSETS

CASH AND CASH EQUIVALENTS					
Type of Account	Where Held	Account Number	Held by H,W, Both	Balance	Notes
Savings or interest bearing accounts					
Checking					
Checking					
Checking					
CDs					
Money Market					
Other:					
TOTAL				$	

INVESTMENT ACCOUNTS AND SECURITIES					
Type of Account	Where Held	Account Number	Held by H,W, Both	Balance	Notes
Stocks					
Bonds					
Other					
Investment Accounts (other than retirement)					
TOTAL				$	

ASSETS (cont)

RETIREMENT ACCOUNTS
(include pension plans, IRAs, defered compensation, annutiies, 401(k)s, etc.)

Type of Account	Where Held	Account Number	Owner	Current Value	Beneficiary/ Vested Amount
TOTAL				$	$

EMPLOYEMENT BENEFITS
(include stock options, ESOPs, other deferred compensation plans or employee perks like frequent flyer miles, season tickets, etc.)

Description	Where Held	Account Number	Owner	Number of Shares/Value	Notes
TOTAL				$	

REAL PROPERTY

	Address	Current Market Value	Held by H,W, Both	Mortgage /Loan Holder	Notes
Residence					
Secondary or Vacation					
Investment or Business					
Other *(specify)*					
TOTAL		$			

Appendix A: The Workbook - Assets and Liabilities

ASSETS (cont)

MOTOR VEHICLES					
(include cars, trucks, boats, RVs, etc.)					
Description	Year/Make/Model	Loan Amount	Held by H,W, Both	Current Value	Notes
TOTAL		$		$	

INSURANCE POLICIES					
(include life, disability, property or business policies)					
Description	Holder/Owner	Beneficiary	Insurer / Policy #	Face Value	Cash Value
TOTAL				$	$

BUSINESS INTERESTS					
linclude corporations, partnerships, sole proprietorships)					
Name	Address	Held by H,W, Both	% of Ownership	Current Value	Notes
TOTAL				$	

LIABILITIES

PRIMARY RESIDENCE		Address:			
	Mortgage /Loan Holder	Account Number	Held by H,W, Both	Balance Due	Monthly Payment
Mortgage					
Home Equity Loan					
Line of Credit					
Other					
TOTAL				$	$

VACATION OR INVESTMENT PROPERTY		Address:			
	Mortgage /Loan Holder	Account Number	Held by H,W, Both	Balance Due	Monthly Payment
Mortgage(s)					
Home Equity Loan(s)					
Line(s) of Credit					
Other					
TOTAL				$	$

CAR LOANS					
Description	Loan Holder	Account Number	Held by H,W, Both	Balance Due	Monthly Payment
TOTAL				$	$

Appendix A: The Workbook - Assets and Liabilities

LIABILITIES (cont)

STUDENT LOANS

Description	Loan Holder	Account Number	Held by H,W, Both	Balance Due	Monthly Payment
TOTAL				$	$

OTHER LOANS

Description	Loan Holder	Account Number	Held by H,W, Both	Balance Due	Monthly Payment
TOTAL				$	$

CREDIT CARD DEBT

Description	Credit Card Provider	Account Number	Held by H,W, Both	Balance Due	Monthly Payment
TOTAL				$	$

Instructions: Make copies for each room in the house

HOUSEHOLD INVENTORY WORKSHEET

Room _____ (e.g., Living Room, Master Bedroom, Kitchen, etc.)

Item	Description (Serial # if applicable)	Quantity	Purchased during marriage?	Current value (approx.)	Who is keeping?		
					Her	Him	Dispute

Watch Video Message: Patricia Stallworth
- Before You Sign

www.psworth.com/divorceworkbook

BEFORE YOU SIGN THE FINAL PAPERS CHECKLIST

Before you sign the final papers, be sure that your divorce decree contains all of the pertinent information to protect you. Here is a checklist to help you review them:

Property

- ☐ Who gets what property?
- ☐ Who gets which debts?
- ☐ If a pension is to be divided, has a QDRO been completed so that the pension is now divided and in the appropriate names?
- ☐ If you are transferring property to your spouse has your name been removed either through refinancing or payment of the debt so that you are no longer liable?
- ☐ If there is a property settlement note, is it collateralized? In other words, are there other assets to back it up in the case of non-payment? Is interest included in the payments?

Child Support and Custody

- ☐ Who has custody of the children?
- ☐ What is the visitation schedule?

Child Support and Custody (cont.)

- ☐ How much child support will you receive and for how long?
- ☐ Will the child support change during college or when visitation changes?
- ☐ Who pays related expenses for school (transportation, books, etc.) and unusual expenses (lessons, camp, braces, etc.)?
- ☐ Who pays related expenses for school (transportation, books, etc.) and unusual expenses (lessons, camp, braces, etc.)?
- ☐ Who will deduct the children on income tax forms?*

*Note the 2017 tax law changes eliminated deductions for dependents.

Alimony

- ☐ How much alimony will you receive and for how long?
- ☐ Is life insurance / disability in place to cover alimony in the event of your spouse's death or disability?
- ☐ If alimony is not awarded now, can it be awarded later?

Miscellaneous

- ☐ Compare copies of your credit report before your divorce and now to determine if anything has changed. Look for new debts, items you don't recognize and get that cleared up first especially if it looks your soon-to-be ex has added debt that you may be liable for.
- ☐ Who pays legal fees?

Miscellaneous (cont.)

- ☐ Will the husband pay the legal fees and court costs related to non-payment of alimony/child support or not complying with the divorce decree? Will interest charges be imposed?
- ☐ If you have requested it, is the process to revert to your maiden name in place?
- ☐ Make sure that all insurance (health, home, auto and life) is addressed and reviewed.
- ☐ Review wills and beneficiaries on accounts for necessary changes.
- ☐ Keep a journal of all visitation and support payments.

Note: If your spouse files for bankruptcy and it will impact payments to you or to creditors that you could then be liable for, contact a lawyer as soon as possible.

AFTER DIVORCE CHECKLIST

It is so important to follow up on any details after your divorce so that they do not continue to haunt you. Here are some basic things to do.

- ☐ Make several copies of your Judgment or Decree and Marital Settlement Agreement because you may need them for any transfer of property, accounts, debts, etc.
- ☐ Check to see that your "Certificate of Divorce or Dissolution of Marriage" has been filed with the Clerk's Office.
- ☐ Check to see that all necessary documents have been filed with the child support enforcement office.
- ☐ Make sure all joint accounts are closed and distributed accordingly. But first be sure there are not any outstanding checks.
- ☐ If you made any arrangements with any company for automatic withdrawals or payments, be sure you contact them prior to closing accounts.
- ☐ Make sure all property is distributed properly. If arrangements need to be made for pick-ups or drop-offs, do it as soon as possible, so you do not forget anything.
- ☐ If there were automobiles to be transferred, be sure to take care of the title, registration and license plates.
- ☐ If there was real estate involved in the Marital Settlement Agreement, be sure to take care of the deed work and any necessary mortgage changes.

- ☐ Make sure that all insurance (health, home, auto and life) is addressed and reviewed.
- ☐ Review wills and beneficiaries on accounts for necessary changes.
- ☐ Keep a journal of all visitation and support payments.

Note: If your spouse files for bankruptcy and it will impact payments to you or to creditors that you could then be liable for, contact a lawyer as soon as possible.

Watch Video Message: Patricia Stallworth
- Next Steps

www.psworth.com/divorceworkbook

APPENDIX B: GLOSSARY

action: The legal name for a lawsuit.

affidavit: A written factual statement sworn to under oath.

agreement: A written document setting out areas of agreement, signed by the parties and their lawyers.

alimony: Money paid to a former spouse for his or her support; same as maintenance or spousal maintenance.

allegation: A statement by one of the parties as to what he or she believes – and intends to prove – is true.

appeal: A challenge to a court decision by taking the case to another, higher court.

arbitration: A form of dispute resolution in which parties submit issues to a third party who decided how they should be resolved; can be binding or nonbinding.

brief: A written argument of facts and law, with references to other relevant decisions, submitted by a lawyer at trial or on appeal.

chambers: A judge's office.

collaborative law: A form of alternate dispute resolution in which the lawyers agree that they will put their energies into selling the case. If they are unsuccessful, they will withdraw and other lawyers will take the case to trial.

community property: The name given to property acquired during a marriage in community property states, which refers to the property as belonging to the married couple.

contempt: Disobeying a court order.

counterclaim: A response to claims made in the complaint or petition.

court reporter: A person who takes down what is said at a trial, motion or deposition. The court reporter will provide a transcript of the matter upon request.

custody: The care and upbringing of the children of divorce.

custody evaluation: A study conducted by trained professional – social workers, psychologists or child development experts – to make recommendations to the court about a custody arrangement that is in the children's best interests.

decision: The judge's conclusions in a case; includes the judge's reasoning and how the judge saw the facts.

default: A hearing at which only one side appears, either because an agreement has been reached before the hearing or because one side does not show up despite having notice of the hearing.

defendant: One who defends against a lawsuit brought against him or her by the plaintiff. *(See respondent.)*

deposition: The testimony of a potential witness to a trial taken out of court and under oath. The deposition is ordinarily transcribed into a document for later use.

discovery: Gathering information needed for settling or trying the divorce case.

dissolution: The current word for divorce.

domestic violence: When one member of a household causes harm, makes threats of harm or acts in a way to create fear or harm against another household member.

emancipation: When parents are no longer legally responsible for the children. Parents are legally responsible for their children until the kids reach a certain age (18-21 in most states), marry, join the military or choose to live independently.

equitable: Reasonable under the circumstances. Usually refers to property division.

evidence: The information provided to the court at trial or the information used by the parties and lawyers to reach an agreement.

ex parte: When one side goes to a judge for relief, usually in an emergency. Most states require the party seeking relief to notify the other, who may choose whether to appear in response.

expert: A person with specialized knowledge about issues within the divorce.

forensic accountant: A person retained to analyze, interpret, summarize and present complex financial and business related issues.

garnishment: Collection of money – child support and alimony – from a paycheck by a governmental agency that then forwards payments according to existing court orders.

grounds: The legal basis for claiming that the marriage is over. This may be marital misconduct, incompatibility or irretrievable breakdown. Some states require the parties to have lived apart for a specific period of time ranging from 90 days to two years.

guardian ad litem: Also called law guardian. A lawyer appointed by the court – usually paid for by the parties – to provide information about what custodial arrangement would be in the best children's best interests.

hearing: An appearance before the court at which evidence is produced and arguments are made.

hold harmless: One of the parties agrees to be responsible for a debt and protects the other from any expenses or losses related to the debt collection.

indemnification: To promise to reimburse another person if he or she suffers harm or loss; same as *hold harmless*.

interim order: Same as *temporary order*.

interlocutory decree: A judgement of the court this is not final until a specified time has elapsed. During this period the parties are not free to marry again.

joint custody: When the parties share responsibility for child rearing.

joint legal custody: When the parties make major decisions about their children's education, medical care and religious upbringing together.

joint petition: When people getting divorced are in agreement from the outset, they may prepare a joint petition for dissolution that sets out the facts and a stipulation that sets out their agreements. Both parties sign this document and papers do not need to be served.

joint physical custody: When parents share physical care of their children. While the time division need not be 50-50, it is usually close to that.

judgement: A court order based on the parties' agreement or following a trial on the issues.

judgement and decree: The document that says the parties are divorced and contains the court's decisions on issues before it.

legal custody: Parental decision-making about the children's education, medical care and religious upbringing.

legal separation: Also called separate maintenance. Some people don't want a divorce (often for religious or financial reasons) but need a court order setting rules for their behavior. They may seek a decree of legal separation that addresses custody and support. The decree does not dissolve the marriage.

litigation: Bringing issues to court and presenting them in the form required by the rules.

maintenance: See *alimony*.

marital property: The property acquired by the parties during the marriage not by gift or inheritance. This property is subject to division in divorce.

mediation: A form of dispute resolution in which the parties meet with a third person, a mediator to resolve their differences. The mediator cannot give legal advice.

negotiations: The communications among the parties and their lawyers as they work to resolve the issues.

no-fault divorce: The rule in most states today. It is not necessary to prove an irretrievable breakdown of the marriage has occurred or that one of the parties is at fault.

non-custodial parent: The parent with whom the children do not live.

non-marital property: Property acquired before the marriage or by inheritance or gift.

order: A written court decision directing behavior. An order can be based on an agreement of the parties or a court decision after a contested hearing.

order for protection: An order issued in a domestic violence matter that directs one party to stay away from the other and not to harm that person. Violating an order for protection is a basis for arrest and criminal charges.

parenting plan: The actual practical arrangement worked out by the parties that says when each will provide care and take responsibility for the children.

petition: Also called complaint. This document, together with a summons, begins a divorce. It sets out the facts required by state statutes and asks the court to grant certain things.

petitioner: The party who initiates the divorce; also called the plaintiff.

physical custody: The actual hands-on care of the children.

plaintiff: See *petitioner*.

pro per or pro se: Acting as your own attorney.

respondent: The person who responds to the divorce papers served by the petitioner. If the initiator is called the plaintiff, then the responder is called the defendant.

settlement: An agreement reached by negotiation.

sole custody: One parent is responsible for the children.

sole legal custody: One parent makes all of the decisions about education, medical care and religious upbringing.

sole physical custody: One parent provides most of the actual child care.

stock options: The right to purchase shares of stock in the company at a specific price after a specific holding period. Often part of an executive's bonus package.

summons: The initiating document of a divorce that requires a response in 30 days and usually contains restraining orders governing behavior and assets.

temporary order: Also called an interim order. An order issued during a divorce to set rules until a divorce is final.

trial: A contested hearing before a judge.

visitation: The time spent by a non-custodial parent with their children.

APPENDIX C: RESOURCES

LEGAL

American Academy of Matrimonial Lawyers 312-263-6477 www.aaml.org

Association for Conflict Resolution (mediators and arbitrators)   202-464-9700 www.acrnet.org

International Academy of Collaborative Professionals   415-897-2398 www.collabgroup.com

Legal Aid 202-259-1500 www.lsc.gov/what-legal-aid/find-legal-aid

Legal Information Institute (link to state divorce laws): www.law.cornell.edu/topics/Table_Divorce.htm

State Bar Associations:

- Alabama 334-269-1515 www.alabar.org

- Alaska 907-272-7469 www.alaskabar.org

- Arkansas 800-609-5668 www.arkbar.com

- Arizona 866-482-9227 www.azbar.org

- California 415-538-2000 www.calbar.ca.gov

- Colorado 303-860-1115 www.cobar.org

- Connecticut 860-223-4400 www.ctbar.org

- Delaware 302-658-5279 www.dsba.org

- District of Columbia 202-737-4700 www.dcbar.org 202-223-6600 www.badc.org

- Florida 850-561-5600 www.floridabar.org

Appendix C: Resources

State Bar Associations (cont.)

- Georgia 800-334-6865 www.gabar.org
- Hawaii 808-537-1868 www.hsba.org
- Idaho 208-334-4500 www2.state.id.us
- Illinois 800-252-8908 www.isba.org
- Indiana 800-266-2581 www.inbar.org
- Iowa 515-243-3179 www.iowabar.org
- Kansas 785-234-5696 www.ksbar.org
- Kentucky 502-564-3795 www.kybar.org
- Louisiana 504-566-1600 www.lsba.org
- Maine 207-622-7523 www.mainebar.org
- Maryland 800-492-1964 www.msba.org
- Massachusetts 617-338-0500 www.massbar.org
- Michigan 800-968-1442 www.michbar.org
- Minnesota 800-882-6722 www.mnbar.org
- Mississippi 601-948-4471 www.msbar.org
- Missouri 573-635-4128 www.mobar.org
- Montana 406-442-7660 www.montanabar.org
- Nebraska 800-927-0117 www.nebar.com
- Nevada 702-382-2200 www.nvbar.org
- New Hampshire 603-224-6942 www.nhbar.org
- New Jersey 732-249-5000 www.njbar.org
- New Mexico 505-797-6000 www.nmbar.org
- New York 518-463-3200 www.nysba.org

State Bar Associations (cont.)

- North Carolina 800-662-7407 www.ncbar.org
- North Dakota 701-255-1404 www.sband.org
- Ohio 800-282-6556 www.ohiobar.org
- Oklahoma 405-416-7000 www.okbar.org
- Oregon 800-452-8260 www.osbar.org
- Pennsylvania 717-238-6715 www.pa-bar.org
- Puerto Rico 787-721-3358 www.capr.org
- Rhode Island 401-421-5740 www.ribar.com
- South Carolina 803-799-6653 www.scbar.org
- South Dakota 800-952-2333 www.sdbar.org
- Tennessee 615-383-7421 www.tba.org
- Texas 800-204-2222 www.texasbar.com
- Utah 801-531-0600 www.utahbar.org
- Vermont 802-223-2020 www.vtbar.org
- Virginia 804-775-0500 www.vsb.org 804-644-0041 www.vba.org
- Washington 800-945-9722 www.wsba.org
- West Virginia 304-558-2456 www.wvbar.org
- Wisconsin 800-728-7788 www.wisbar.org
- Wyoming 307-632-9061 www.wyomingbar.org

FINANCIAL

American Institute of CPAs 888-777-7077 www.aicpa.org

Institute for Divorce Financial Analysts (CDFA) 800-875-1760 www.institutedfa.com

Certified Financial Planners (CFP) 800-487-1497 www.cfp.net

National Association of Personal Financial Advisors 847-483-5400 www.napfa.org

Institute of Business Appraisers 984-584-1144 www.go-iba.org

Internal Revenue Service 800-829-1040 www.irs.gov Alimony requirements: www.irs.gov/taxtopics/tc452.html Exemption form: www.irs.gov/pub/irs-pdf/f8332.pdf

National Association of Forensic Accountants 800-267-2130 www.nafanet.com

National Foundation for Consumer Credit 800-388-2227 www.nfcc.org

Social Security Administration 800-772-1213 www.ssa.gov

OTHER SERVICES

Certified Divorce Coaches 813-455-1134 www.certifieddivorcecoach.com

American Association for Marriage and Family Therapy (AAMFT) 703-838-9808 www.aamft.org/iMIS15/AAMFT

Mediation.Org 877-250-0329 www.mediation.org

Domestic Violence Hotline: www.thehotline.org 800-799- SAFE (7233)

ABOUT THE AUTHOR

Patricia Stallworth is a money coach and strategist, an empowerment activist and the founder of the MYM365 Club – a business and financial community.

She is an author of several books including Minding Your Money, the host of the Minding Your Money 360° Podcast and a former instructor in the CFP® and CDFA (Certified Divorce Financial Analyst) Programs at Oglethorpe University.

Prior to starting her own firm, she worked in a management or advisory capacity with several firms, including Deloitte & Touche, the Small Business Development Center, American Express Financial Advisors and AXA Financial.

Patricia has been entertaining audiences for over a decade with her honest, direct and sometimes irreverent talk about money.

Contact: info@psworth.com

www.psworth.com/about-patricia

ABOUT MINDING YOUR MONEY

No matter what situation you find yourself in — going through a divorce, planning for retirement, working to get out of debt, or planning a better life for your family — *minding your money* is important so that you can ride out the challenges and take advantage of opportunities that come your way.

Minding Your Money is based on the principle that earning money is simply not enough — you must also *mind your money*. And, that means taking an active role in managing what comes in, what goes out and where it goes so that it moves you closer to where you want to be.

Achieving financial freedom is a combination of:

- Developing *income streams* so that money is always coming in from various sources.

- *Minding your money elements* such as...
    - A powerful vision for your life that motivates you
    - Goals and a plan to achieve your vision that directs your money in ways that works for you
    - A wealthy mindset that works for you so you stay on track to achieve your goals.

Even though this process to achieve financial freedom is relatively simple, many people never achieve it.

It's a proven fact that changing your relationship with money can change your future! And, that's our mission -- to transform people's lives by helping them change their relationship with money.

Visit www.psworth.com or contact Patricia (info@psworth.com) to learn how we might be able to help you

"Minding your money — the path to a richer life." — Patricia Stallworth

Divorce Consulting

Money is often a big issue in marriages and it becomes even more so during the divorce process.

Divorce can mean a significant financial transition for you. It can be a time of uncertainty and unease about the future. We help by providing answers to your *burning* questions as well as divorce planning advice to help clients understand the impact of the financial decisions they make during the divorce settlement process.

This can include:

- Developing a snapshot of present spending, earnings and assets
- Creating a future plan for your life after divorce
- Analyzing possible divisions of property and divorce settlement scenarios

For more information: Contact Patricia at info@psworth.com

THANK YOU!!

Thank you for purchasing this book. Please do not hesitate to contact us if you have questions or suggestions. Your feedback and reviews are so important because it helps us improve and it helps others decide if this would be a good book for them. So, if you found the information presented here helpful, please take a moment to leave a review, or contact us directly at info@psworth.com.

Visit my website: PSWorth.com and sign up to receive free helpful tips and get the latest information about upcoming classes, new tools and training. Also, connect with me:

LinkedIn: Patricia Stallworth

Twitter: PatStallworth

Facebook: MindingYourMoney

YouTube Channel: PatriciaStallworth

Minding Your Money Books:

Minding Your Money: Personal, Money Management and Investment Strategies

The Minding Your Money Handbook: Simple Strategies to Take Charge of Your Money to Create the Life You Want

Minding Your Money: 27 Savvy Financial Strategies for Women

www.ingramcontent.com/pod-product-compliance
Lightning Source LLC
Chambersburg PA
CBHW060514300426
44112CB00017B/2662